CATCH A STAR

Shining through Adversity
to Become a Champion

TAMIKA CATCHINGS

WITH KEN PETERSEN

Revell

a division of Baker Publishing Group
Grand Rapids, Michigan

Published by Revell
a division of Baker Publishing Group
P.O. Box 6287, Grand Rapids, MI 49516-6287
www.revellbooks.com

Printed in the United States of America

Library of Congress Cataloging-in-Publication Data is on file at the Library of Congress, Washington, DC.

ISBN 978-0-8007-2368-2

Published in association with the literary agency of Legacy, LLC, Winter Park, FL 32789.

16 17 18 19 20 21 22   7 6 5 4 3 2 1

CONTENTS

Contents

FOREWORD

I was the head coach of the Indianapolis Colts for seven years, and during that time I had the privilege of working with some tremendous athletes. Our 2006 Colts team brought the city a Super Bowl title and featured players who will one day be voted into the NFL Hall of Fame. But it would probably surprise people to know that the most decorated athlete in the city of Indianapolis at that time didn't play for the Colts. Most people would guess Peyton Manning of the Colts, and if not Peyton, then Reggie Miller of the Pacers. But as great as those two were, and as much as they did for the city, their accomplishments in the athletic arena did not match up to those of Tamika Catchings.

Tamika played on a State Championship high school basketball team and an NCAA National Championship team at the University of Tennessee. She won a WNBA title with the Indiana Fever and has been named MVP of the league, MVP of the Championship Series, as well as Defensive Player of the Year. Tamika has represented the United States in international competition as well, and has won three Olympic gold medals. In fact, I don't know an athlete who has accomplished as much in his or her sport as Tamika Catchings has in women's basketball.

Detailing her achievements on the court, however, barely scratches the surface of her impact in the city of Indianapolis and all over Central Indiana. Tamika has been a shining light in the community, a tireless worker, and a tremendous role model for not only young athletes but for everyone. She is one of the rare superstar athletes who really "get it." As a Christian athlete, Tamika understands she has been gifted by God and that with this blessing comes responsibility—a responsibility to give back to those in her community, but also a responsibility to let her light shine and point others to Christ.

Getting to know Tamika Catchings was one of the great privileges I had while working in Indianapolis. During my time there I got to see her interact with people at games, charity functions, and events for her Catch the Stars Foundation. I also got to see her away from the crowds and the lights, simply interacting with young people. And no matter where we were, or who we were with, Tamika was always the same—personable, caring, and humble. She has an amazing ability to be a leader to her teammates on the court, but also to connect with people who look up to her and make them feel comfortable.

At first glance, it would appear that Tamika is one of those people who has been incredibly blessed with God-given talent and who has worked hard to take advantage of her opportunities. While that's true, she has also had to deal with many personal challenges and setbacks. In reading her story you'll learn of some of those obstacles, how she used her faith in Christ to deal with them, and how overcoming those obstacles helped shape Tamika into the person she is today. I believe *Catch a Star* will not only give you a look into Tamika's life but will also inspire you to strive to be all you can be in life as well.

Tony Dungy

I'm sitting on a playground at three years old, and my back is to my dad. He's calling my name. "Tamika . . . Tamika . . ." But I don't hear anything. I'm lost in my sand castle. Lost in my own world. Happiness displayed in my body, my face, and my smile. My dad thought I was ignoring him, but the truth was I did not hear him.

That's the moment my parents started wondering, "Is something wrong with her? Can she truly not hear us?" And then the thought, "Please, Lord, not again." My older brother, Kenyon, had just gone through the same extensive hearing testing I would go through. And in the end, I would be diagnosed with a moderate to severe hearing problem, slightly worse than Kenyon's but causing the same frustration and the beginning of a life of adversity.

Part 1

SILENCE

Lips move . . .
Silence Surrounds . . .
The world flashes by but all I see is movement.
All I hear is silence.
Darkness settles in,
But I am not scared.
Not scared of being alone,
Not scared of the emptiness around.
Not scared of the emotions swirled round in my head.

Though it's dark,
I see light.
And I force my steps into that direction.
I'm guided by a pleasant presence
One not seen, but known.
Welcome to my reality . . .
My life.

1

PLAY

Tamika is just one of those people who could excel at anything she set her mind to. She just works that hard. She could be a Serena Williams, if she had chosen tennis. Well, she chose basketball.

Tauja Catchings

My dad tells about that day. About Tauja and me playing basketball outside in the driveway. About a "friendly" game of one-on-one.

It was our favorite thing, basketball. It was our whole family's favorite thing, even though as a family we enjoyed lots of sports, including soccer and volleyball. But if someone asked the question, "Do you want to play?" no one ever had to ask, "Play what?" That orange basketball was the fiery nucleus our family life spun around.

11

It's almost like there's a basketball gene that our parents passed down to their children. The Catchingses had it, big time—my dad playing in the pros with Dr. J and the 76ers; my older sister, Tauja, eventually playing in college and beyond; and my older brother, Kenyon, playing on his high school team until his dreams for the game were cut short by illness. But more than any of them, I was bound and determined to be a basketball player. Even as a young girl, I knew basketball was going to be *my* game. And, no, it wasn't that I just had lucky genes. A lot of people have physical ability to play—height and agility—but to play well at a high level requires more. Intensity. Desire. Passion. Focus. Determination. Hard work.

Back then, at the age of nine, I didn't have the physique for the game. Not yet. I was small, but really because of my slouching to "blend in." And not only that, but I couldn't hear very well—I'd been born with moderate to severe hearing loss.

But so what if I was skinny and short and couldn't hear much? What I *did* have was intensity. I had desire. And I had passion and a willingness to work hard for the game like no one else in my family.

As Tauja and I played in the driveway that day, we were slamming hard against each other, as we always did. Our game was one of fighting for the ball, defending tough, scraping and scrapping to get the edge and score yet one more basket. I'd sink a basket, and then Tauja would take the ball at the other end of the driveway, dribble it forward, juke and deke to try to get me off-balance, giving her an opening to burst through and slide toward the hoop for a layup. Then I'd have the ball again, walking it up toward my big sister, and I'd feint one way and dribble the other to get around her and score.

12

Later in life my dad would say one reason I got so good was because of all those early years playing against Tauja, who was the best talent around. I think that's right. She made me better. She was a year older, taller than me then, and in my eyes just perfect all around.

All those realities just made me compete harder.

We'd play so physical that we'd sometimes send the other flying, with a yell or a shriek, clearly a foul in any refereed game but perfectly acceptable on the court of our driveway arena. We'd scrape an arm or a knee, wipe off a little blood, and start playing again, yelling and taunting and at times screaming at each other.

My dad tells about that day, how the yelling and screaming got to be too much for him. He could tell we were playing each other hard. He knew there'd been some blood. He'd heard one scream too many. He walked out on the porch and yelled, "That's enough!"

We froze in our tracks. He came out to the driveway, confiscated the ball, and took it inside with him.

Frustrated, Tauja stormed up to her room. I knew she'd probably play with her dolls after she cooled down. Dad settled back down inside.

Sometime later, as Dad tells it, he looked up from his paper and realized Tauja had come into the house, but I hadn't. *Where's Tamika?* he thought.

Looking outside, he saw me still in the driveway. And there I was—playing.

With an imaginary basketball.

He watched me dribble my invisible ball behind my back, through my legs, then toward the basket, where I'd launch myself for an imaginary layup. And I picked up that pretend ball as if it were real and walked it to the back of the driveway. And I'd start all over—dribbling, dodging an imaginary player so I could get free, jump, and shoot my imaginary ball, for an imaginary three-pointer, from beyond an imaginary arc.

I did this again and again. Over and over.

I could *hear* the game in my head.

What I couldn't hear for real, I could hear in another way. The *smack, smack* of the ball as it bounced on concrete, the *slap* of my hand against rubber as I grabbed the ball on the upward bounce, and the oh-so-lovely *swish* as my imaginary shot arced through the air and slipped cleanly between the rim—nothing but net.

In imagining the game, it was like I could sense other players, where they were on the court, even without hearing a thing. It was as if I could hear one player racing stealthily from behind, rushing in from the side to swipe a steal, and I could feel the vibration of his or her thudding feet just in time to grab the ball from my dribble and swing it away.

As I played within my silence, I could dart and weave through the holes in the defense, racing toward the basket. As I jumped, the imaginary ball rolled off my fingertips against the backboard. And it was as if I could hear it, the sound of it banking against the glass, clanging on the rim—once, twice, and more—before finally, finally, finally falling in.

Yes, basketball was my game.

And for the longest time, it was where I could hide and hear what I wanted to hear.

2

DIFFERENT

Could you imagine if somebody traveled back in
time to that moment and went up to us and said,
"Hey, you two are going to be some of the best
basketball players to ever pick up a basketball?"
We'd be like, "What?"

Kobe Bryant, Los Angeles Lakers

I don't know why I thought I might go unnoticed, but I
hoped since our school was brand-new in Abilene, Texas,
no one would make a fuss over how my brother and sister
and I were new too.

It's no use thinking you can slip into obscurity when you
already stand out. I didn't look or talk like the other kids
at Reagan Elementary School. It wasn't just that I was the
new girl from another city. I was the new girl from overseas,

from Italy, and yet not Italian. I was a United States citizen, with a mom from Texas, and yet not at all steeped in Texas culture. The only thing I understood about being in the Lone Star state was being lone.

I wore glasses and these brown, matchbox-sized amplifying devices that fit behind each ear. A light brown plastic casing wrapped over the upper ear lobes and connected with tiny tubes to a clear, bulblike speaker that tucked inside each ear itself. I didn't think much about wearing them. You get used to them, like glasses. I don't remember not having them when I was young, so they were just a normal thing to me. Until other kids made me aware that they weren't. I was the only one in my class with items that made me look so different. I might have been wearing a sign that said "Something's wrong with me." My new classmates noticed, and they weren't about to let anything different go without comment. Kids can be so mean.

"What are those?" kid after kid asked on my first day of second grade. They pointed at my ears.

"Four eyes," another kid said, snickering, pointing at my glasses.

For the first time I realized I was different. I'd worn the big box hearing aids as long as I could remember. My older brother, Kenyon, was also born with moderate hearing loss. It skipped Tauja, just twenty-one months older than me, and she was used to being our ears for us. She would make sure to repeat what we couldn't quite make out and tell us what we never heard.

She became my voice too.

Ever shy, I'd learned to rely on Tauj to speak up for me. I felt completely safe and connected with her. Though we couldn't be more different personality-wise, she understood me and looked out for me. She was the instigator, and I was more of a go-with-the-flow girl. I was prone to think more on something before digging into it, and while Tauj is a thinker too, she's more likely to plunge right in, start a thing by doing it. Where I loved books and reading, was a tomboy, and kept to myself, not speaking much to people I didn't know, Tauja could talk your ear off (and would), and played sports but loved playing with her dolls more.

So early on we became a team, balancing out one another. Where I would hold back, she bounded forward, fearless. Where I didn't want to speak up, she spoke for me. What I couldn't hear, she repeated and passed along. We felt at home with one another.

That was good—because home changed a lot for us.

We had moved across the country and the world almost as fast as the basketball our father, Harvey Catchings, dribbled down the court in the NBA. He played in the league from 1974 to 1985, beginning in Philadelphia for the 76ers, then for the Nets in New Jersey, where I was born, then Milwaukee for the Bucks, and a year in Los Angeles for the Clippers.

When he finished his pro career in the NBA, we all wondered where we were going to go next. We were told we weren't just going to move to another city. We were going to move overseas. And I remember thinking, *There's a world outside of the USA?*

Dad was going to play for an Italian team, Segafredo. We moved to a little town called Gorizia, in the northeast corner of Italy, about a day's drive from Venice. This would be the fourth home I could remember. I was just seven.

The Italian league Dad played in featured some former NBA basketball players, including a guy named Joe who went by the nickname of "Jellybean" who had played with the 76ers the same years Dad had played in Philly, at the beginning of the team's Julius Erving era. Of course, I didn't know much yet about the NBA. I just knew my dad was a great basketball player who'd played with some other guys in the pros—this guy named Jellybean and some doctor. Dr. J.

Jellybean Bryant's family was living there also, and we got to know them well that year. His wife, Pam, was real nice, and they had two girls, Sharia and Shaya. And a boy by the name of Kobe.

Kobe Bryant.

We played with each other. We did sightseeing together. We had so much in common—not only English and being American but we were African American families in a country that didn't have many of "us." Strangers in a strange land, our families developed a close relationship while we were there.

We were in Italy just a year before moving to Abilene. Later I would come to cherish that year and come to think of it as the last time I really felt free. In another time and place my childhood friendship with Kobe Bryant might have seemed pretty awesome to the kids at school in Abilene. But Kobe Bryant wasn't "Kobe" to anyone yet.

And Tamika Catchings was still just an odd-looking girl with big box hearing aids over her ears.

Italy should have made my challenges the next year in Abilene, Texas, less surprising.

In Italy, I'd glimpsed what it was like to be an outsider. I'd begged my parents to let me learn Italian. Kobe spoke Italian. But my real reason was I wanted to understand what Italian people were saying at school and in our neighborhood. But Mom and Dad wanted me to master English first.

Wise enough, I suppose. My hearing disorder had also left me with a bit of a speech problem—a mild lisp, but enough to make me seem even more different to others. Mom and Dad wanted me to get better at speaking English, rather than confuse me with another language.

Once in Abilene, though, my "somewhat better English" didn't help me with the other kids. That's because there was a whole other language to learn here, the language of how to be accepted and acceptable. A language I didn't know. So much of this language is unspoken, and though we're all introduced to it, we can struggle all our lives to make peace with it.

Even though Tauj, in third grade, and Kenyon, in fifth, went to the same school and we sometimes could have lunch together, I mostly felt alone in Abilene.

Teachers didn't help. Within the first couple of weeks of being set apart by other kids for how I looked and talked, I was set apart by the classes too. Someone decided, because I didn't always hear my own voice well and struggled to hear and enunciate certain sounds, like in *ch* and *sh* and *S* words, that I should go to speech therapy class.

The first day the therapist came to our classroom, she walked right in on a lesson, interrupting our teacher, whispering in her ear. My teacher nodded toward me, and all eyes riveted to mine as she announced, "Tamika, you can go now."

Go where? I wondered. I hadn't been told about the speech therapy that would separate me two and three times a week from the other students. I didn't know what to expect as I trailed the speech therapist out of the classroom, but I wanted to melt, disappear from all my classmates' stares.

One boy groaned and asked what all the other kids must have been thinking: "Why do you get out of class?"

If any kids hadn't thought I was so different before this, they did now.

I wound through the desks, past the stares, and down the hall after the speech therapist. I should have welcomed the escape. Instead, I wished I could stay back at my desk, unnoticed, to hear what everyone else was hearing, learn what everyone else was learning. I loved learning at school. I just didn't like being set apart, standing out, and being put down.

Speech therapy classes became another form of weekly torment. The therapist was kind enough, but all through our sessions, she made me repeat certain sounds over and over. It was like she was teaching a baby to speak. Well, I wasn't a baby. All the while I thought of my classmates getting to read books and write whole stories.

The teasing got worse. My wish to fit in became my prayer every new day of second grade in Abilene. Instead of kids getting used to my differences, they got used to tormenting me. One day it was about the glasses; the next, about the speech therapy classes that must have seemed mysterious and secret to them. Later it would be the braces put on my teeth.

Mostly it was about the awkward hearing aids.

I hated those hearing aids. I was grateful for how they enabled me to hear, but I couldn't stand anyone commenting on them or staring at them. I couldn't bear going to school, and then couldn't wait to get home.

I knew Mom would be there. Our mom, Wanda, was always there.

Dinner would be in the making, ready for us after whatever recreational activity we had for the evening. But, she always had a snack ready for us when we got home. She'd sit with us at the table, hear about our day, help with homework, and share in the small victories and challenges that make up grade school: acing a test, getting more homework, dealing with classmates.

Her question was always the same when we walked into the kitchen where she'd be setting out the snacks: "How was school today?"

My response was the same. For three months, the same. "Please, Mom, please. Don't make me go back." I stared down at the table. "The kids say mean things. I can't do that anymore."

"Tamika." She walked over to me and took my chin in her hand, turning my face toward hers. "You know you have to go to school. Ignore the bad things anyone says. You know what they're saying isn't true. There's nothing wrong with you— you'll get through this." She smiled. "You can do anything you set your mind to do and work toward. The sky's the limit."

I leaned my head against her for a minute. I'd heard her loud and clear. Somewhere deep inside I knew what she said was true. I really did believe I could do what I set my mind to do.

I just wished there was a way I could show it and prove myself to the kids at school.

3

LOST

Are you stupid or something? Uh-uh. Slow. She's slow.

Girls in grade school in Abilene, Texas

My stomach kept rumbling knowing that dinner waited for us in the oven. I knew if I just said and did the right thing, right now, we could all go home and dig in. But how? Admitting what I'd done would mean more than a late dinner. I'd be in big trouble.

We fumbled with flashlights in the dark as dusk turned to night. I could make out enough of Mom's face to see she was beginning to realize what I'd known for a while. We weren't going to find anything on this path to and from school.

At least we weren't freezing. November in Abilene was a lot more comfortable than up north.

23

Mom glared at me again, then went back to her desperate search. My lost hearing aids were expensive. Very expensive. Her unspoken thought, *keep looking*, made me feel even deeper pangs of guilt. I turned my own flashlight onto the grass again, scouring it for what I knew we wouldn't find.

Earlier that afternoon, coming home from school, I'd lagged behind Kenyon and Tauja, crying the whole way after another day in another week of relentless teasing and torment at school. Kenyon and Tauj joked around ahead of me as I got more and more upset, but Tauja glanced back every now and then to check on me. She knew I was upset. The name-calling, the put-downs, all the being singled out and set apart was too much. I hated those big box hearing aids. No one else had to wear them, and even though they did enable me to hear, the way they looked made me feel like an alien or something.

On the walk home from school, I pulled them from my ears, wadded them into a ball, and threw them as far as I could into the grassy vacant lot.

They never weighed much, and though I was used to wearing them, it still felt like a big weight taken off my shoulders to get rid of those hearing aids. Taking them off, tossing them, I felt suddenly lighter. Free.

At home, Mom had our usual snack waiting and I was hungry. I dug into the food and my homework the same way. The whole day seemed better. I hadn't smiled this much after school since we'd moved to Abilene. I plowed through my homework with a renewed mission. After our homework was finished, we headed to the field for softball practice. I loved playing catcher and left field. The day's torment was beginning to fade a bit as I thought about how much I loved pretty much every sport, being outside, running, getting dirty. I was a tomboy, and the field was where I felt most at home.

Mom eyed me all through practice. I knew why.

"What's different about you, Tamika?" Mom stood in front of me, studying my face.

I waggled my head, smiling. "I don't know." Maybe being happy would be enough to keep Mom from figuring it out.

"Tamika," she said as we all piled into the car, "I just can't place it, but something looks different about you."

I watched her face. Even with the hearing aids I sometimes read lips. I shrugged my shoulders. *Act cool*, I told myself. "I don't know," I told Mom.

The truth was I did know, but I wanted to buy more time. I didn't want to give up this freedom, for once, of not being different from everyone else.

Mom looked straight at me and gasped. "Tamika! It's your hearing aids. That's it. That's what's different. You don't have on your hearing aids. Where are they?"

Busted.

"Oh my goodness . . ." I felt around each ear, acting surprised. *Play along.* "I don't know." That was technically true. I didn't know, not exactly. They were somewhere in that vacant lot of tall grass. I just didn't know *exactly* where.

"Where did you last have them in?"

"I remember them on the whole day at school. I must have lost them."

"Lost them?" Mom jumped out of the car and grabbed my hand. She was mad. She pulled me toward the field, yelling over her shoulder for Kenyon and Tauja to follow. "Well, we're going to find them. I want you to think of everywhere you went today."

I knew my hearing aids weren't there, but I followed. It seemed Mom wasn't entirely sure whether or not I knew what happened to the hearing aids, but she was determined to find them. The field grass had been dry and hot hours before practice, but now, as dusk settled in, it was cool with the impending dew. I knew neither the damp grass nor the cracked clay of the infield could give away secrets they didn't hold.

If those hearing aids had gotten knocked off without me noticing, it made the most sense that it would have happened while playing softball. After a while, though, my stomach rumbling louder and louder, I wanted to stop playing along with the search. But I couldn't.

Eventually we packed back into the car and headed home. All I could think about was dinner, but as we jumped out of the car, Mom told us to grab flashlights. "We aren't giving up yet. Let's retrace your steps to and from school."

"Do you remember falling?" Mom kept searching for answers as much as the hearing aids. "Could they have been knocked out on the way home from school?"

"No . . ." I wondered if she was putting together what happened and she spoke as if reading my thoughts.

"Tamika, you know where those hearing aids are. They don't just fall off."

I tried to look innocent and concerned and cool all at the same time, studying the ground between the sidewalk and the street. My hearing aids required a careful process to put on and properly take off. Mom knew it, but I think she was desperate.

We walked back home, passing the lot with the tall grass a second time. I scoured the sides of the walkway. Of course, nothing.

I walked over to Mom, who looked ready to give in too. She straightened up from searching the ground and stood in front of me to ask (for what must have been the thirtieth time) if I could mentally retrace my steps from the entire afternoon. I was tired, but still not ready to give up the truth. "Mom, I don't know exactly where I went." I was careful to keep my exasperation in check. Neither of my parents tolerated a lack of respect. I looked to Tauja. "I was right behind them," I said. "We came home the same way as always." Tauja was playing cool about this. If she knew, she wasn't going to give up my secret.

"Well, I don't think we're going to find them here." The resignation in Mom's voice was clear, all the anger and frustration turned to disappointment, and something else too: worry. She turned slightly away and was talking to herself as much as me when she said, "It doesn't make sense. Softball practice seems like the likeliest place you would have noticed them coming off."

I didn't like seeing her so upset, not telling the whole truth, knowing I was the reason we were all out here in the dark missing dinner. I knew by daylight I could probably find my hearing aids in the vacant lot of tall field grass. I knew the general direction I'd thrown them. To not say so wasn't like me. This had gone on long enough. I had to set things straight, even though I knew I was going to be in big, big trouble.

"Mom, I—"

She never heard me. I stopped as she turned. "Tamika, we can't replace them right now, not yet. We'll just keep looking tomorrow." She hesitated, a tinge of the frustration back in her voice. She knew I understood how expensive the hearing aids were—she and Dad had always been on me to be careful with them, take care of them, put them in the same spot every night before I went to bed. "C'mon," she said, nodding to me and Tauja. "Let's go eat dinner." We turned toward the house and she gave one more admonition before we fell into silence. "For now, Tamika, you're just going to have to do your best without hearing aids. Do you understand me? Do you think you can manage to do without?"

If Mom meant this as punishment for what she decided was carelessness, if not an outright defiance, it wasn't working. Taking away the one thing that set me apart from a physical standpoint gave me one more way to fit in with everyone else, and it gave me hope. School tomorrow might not be so bad.

Yes, I nodded. In fact, I truly felt guilty for what I'd done. Every worry line on Mom's face etched into me the awareness of the importance to her and Dad of the hearing aids, their cost and purpose in helping me overcome my disability. But they didn't know—and no one knew, except perhaps Tauja—how they had made me the target of kids' ridicule.

And maybe even then, at that young age, I was making a decision about my life. I wasn't going to let others tell me who I was. I wasn't some lost, stupid, disabled kid. I had thoughts, feelings, and abilities.

I smiled in the darkness.

"Huh?" I looked from face to face on the playground. Three girls stared, blank, bored, unbelieving, eyebrows raised in question.

I tried again, smiling. "What?"

"Don't you pay attention? Don't you ever listen? How many times do we have to repeat ourselves?"

"Are you stupid or something? Uh-uh. Slow. She's slow."

I hadn't worn the hearing aids for at least a week and no one seemed to notice, not these kids who picked on me for needing the devices, not my teachers. But I was far from getting my wish to fit in. One problem going away just opened the door to another. The hearing aids that drew the most stares and meanest remarks were gone, but the taunts, the digs, still sounded loud and clear. The meanness on some kids' faces, the sneers and stares, spoke volumes too.

I'm sure Mom called and searched for my hearing aids more than I did—calling up to the school, circling the softball field, and more than likely walking the path to and from school. So, I wouldn't dare now to ask Mom and Dad for new devices, but I was struggling more than ever to hear. Even when focused and face-to-face, having a one-on-one conversation was a challenge if there were other people and noise in the background. The creak of swings, slap of jump ropes, bounce of balls on the cement, kids' squeals and yelling—all typical playground noise—became an indistinguishable whirr. I couldn't distinguish any one sound from all the others, not even the voice closest to me, in order to focus.

So like anyone says when they know they've missed something, I asked "Huh?" and "What?" a lot. After a while I started to smile and laugh at what I couldn't quite make out but knew was said to or about me. For a while, that worked. Then it became one more thing for the bullies to pick on.

I'd traded one "different" for another "different."

That the other kids thought I wasn't smart, or was disengaged, hurt the most. I didn't understand why something I couldn't help should be such a matter of conversation or focus.

Stupid? Slow? Not listening? I was none of these things.

Something inside me shifted. I wasn't going to let those labels or anyone else define me. I would show people who I was; I'd prove to them what I could do. I began then what I still do now when I'm faced with a challenge. I dug in with determination. I adjusted. I worked harder. I prayed. I took each of these steps, one at a time.

I figured out a way to go through school on mute.

Even with hearing aids, I'd always compensated a bit by consciously observing more and reading lips. In those first couple of weeks without devices, I became proficient. I watched people's mouths and expressions. I learned to read the curl of a lip, the furrow of a brow. I became hyperaware watching body language, looking for cues and clues. If other kids slammed their textbooks shut, I knew the teacher must have said this lesson was done, or the bell had rung for recess. If they shuffled papers, I could tell it was time to turn in homework or switch to something new.

I sat in the front row. There, I could hear somewhat clearly and I could see the teacher better to read her lips. This worked fine until she turned to write on the chalkboard or get items from her desk. I studied the chalkboard, gripped my pencil, ready to catch whatever was needed. I looked around, tried to see what other kids were writing, get some indicator of where we were going next.

You can guess how that worked. My notebooks told the story. There were pages and pages of meticulous, lengthy notes, then long blank stretches, the places where the teacher had turned and I missed what she said. I looked at those blank spots and knew I had to fill in the gaps, so I stayed after class. I asked the teacher to go over lessons and fill in what I'd missed. I made sure I understood, and asked about what we'd study the next day too.

My teacher loved a student being careful and engaged, diligent and mindful. I don't think she knew these were coping devices, a way of making up for the lost hearing aids. I was glad she liked my efforts, but my goal wasn't to get into her good graces. I wanted to learn and get ahead—getting ahead was my way of keeping up.

One of the best getting-ahead tools I discovered was how to anticipate. I had to make a plan for what to do about the silences and gaps. So I began to come to school early, prepared for what was ahead as a way of getting through. Because I loved to read, I read multiple chapters in the textbooks prior to my classes the next day. I never looked at this as a chore. Reading ahead inspired me to check out library books that related to what we were studying. A lot of these books fed my curiosity, too, so I often read widely on various topics. I asked a lot of questions in and out of the classroom. I had Mom and Tauj go over homework with me. If there was an extra credit opportunity, I took it.

I realized, despite all the teasing and bullying, that I really did love school. I loved learning. I was curious. Challenges motivated me.

So my teachers never really knew my struggles to hear—not my second-grade teacher, nor teachers through the rest of grade school, middle school, and high school. No one asked where the hearing aids I wore at the start of school had gone. To my knowledge there was never any record on file of needing a hearing device, no notes from speech therapy evaluations. It was as if the hearing aids and my hearing problem never existed.

How different my life might be if there were records and notes, if I hadn't thrown those devices into the vacant lot, if something more had been made of the struggles.

But I paid a price. I had to work harder. I had to become more diligent. I had to dig into life. And when I did so, God helped me discover tools that would not only get me through school but help me excel in my learning and then help me achieve so much in basketball. And life.

God took my mess and made it into a miracle.

During my second-grade year, Dad became involved with the Little City Foundation, which provided innovative and personalized programs and services to children and adults with autism and developmental struggles. The foundation was located near Chicago in Deerfield, Illinois.

And then, suddenly, the most wonderful thing happened. Dad's new opportunity meant that we'd have to move once again.

I couldn't wait. Before the end of the school year, we started packing and planning the move out of Abilene.

I began to think how much better Chicago would be than Abilene. Anything would be better for me than Abilene. I was sure I'd not only be leaving Texas but all the teasing and taunting behind me. I wasn't going to be picked on for those big box hearing aids in Chicago. But there were my glasses to contend with still, and soon I would be getting braces on my teeth. And I still struggled to hear and was extremely self-conscious about how I sounded when I talked, though I couldn't always hear myself.

But these wouldn't be the greatest pressures to come. Sometimes the toughest battles are those we never hear coming.

Sports had become the one area of life where I wasn't so miserable. On the court, in the field, at the park, even in the driveway, I could fit in without fear or question. I was at home playing basketball—or any other sport, for that matter.

When I was in third grade, Mom and Dad signed up Tauja and me for our first basketball team at the Deerfield Park District. I was so excited! My first real team . . . *and* with my sister. We walked into practice that first day to be greeted by our new team, mostly boys (I think I remember a couple of other girls), and us. Dad was the coach. I don't remember if that even bothered me. I was there to showcase my skills. Playing in the neighborhood, I'd already discovered I excelled on a basketball court. I could speak and hear its language like no other.

And if I could be really good at basketball, perhaps it would be my way of besting those who made fun of me. Just possibly, if I worked hard enough at the game, it could be my salvation.

The more I played basketball, the more I realized how my hearing loss became my secret weapon. The more sports I engaged in, the more I understood that all the learning and coping techniques I used in the classroom would also pay off in basketball.

Basketball is a sign language, after all. Not only the intentional head nods and hand signals, but the unintentional body language of players in motion that told my searching eyes what the player would do. I learned to read the subtle signs and signals of a player dribbling down the court or behind the line, passing the ball, and making the shot.

On defense, I learned to look around to see if someone needed my attention. I might not be able to hear what a teammate was yelling, but I could see what was coming. I learned then so many adjustments that I use in the game now: keep alert, watch, look around and over your shoulders, check and recheck from side to side. When I was in the game, my head was always moving to see what was going on, what my team captain or coach was doing or saying from the sidelines. I was learning to dial into my surroundings and to focus no matter what the swirl of sound—a crowd or music or players—around me.

Basketball became my escape. Basketball became my voice. And basketball became my home.

I began to challenge some of the kids who teased me to take their issues onto the court. I knew I could win with the ball and the hoop, and there was a little less teasing afterward.

Basketball helped me make some friends in the neighborhood. They may not have understood my struggles, but I had their respect on the court. I could dribble faster, jump higher, and shoot more accurately than most of them. Born with the hearing loss that naturally disconnected me from life and with a shyness that made friendships less likely, I longed for connection. And now, because of basketball, some kids were hanging out with me.

I shot hoops every chance I got. On the court, I functioned very well without the hearing aids. And our dad *did* teach us about the game, although I never remembered a time saying or thinking, *Our dad is famous.* When I got older, yes, there were some opportunities that came our way as kids because of Dad having played in the NBA and his later role working with the NBA Retired Players Association. But—and I think this is cool—there was never one moment when I thought, *Pay attention to how we play the game 'cause my dad's a pro.* No, he was just my dad.

And even if there were some opportunities for me, there certainly were no advantages. In basketball at the college and pro levels, your only "opportunity" is what you do on the court. Your success doesn't come from a dad or older siblings or friends. It's all about you being your best self in playing the game.

And even then, I always wanted to be the *best me* on that court.

That doesn't mean I wanted to speak up, though. I was still self-conscious about how I sounded talking without my hearing aids, unable to hear the sound of my own voice. And this played a big part in my relationship with Tauja. We established a kind of barter system in our friendship.

Early on, Tauja played basketball because she was good at it, but really we were quite different. She was more of a girly-girl than I was. Where I'd rather slide home through the dirt, dust, or mud on the softball field, she loved playing with dolls. Where I loved getting grass burns on my knees in soccer, Tauja preferred to keep clean and play dress up or tool round the neighborhood on her bike.

That often made me cringe, especially when she would beg, "Tamika, would you please play dolls with me? Pleeease?" I'd give her the look that said *don't even ask* because I hated playing dolls. I truly did. I'd do anything to get out of it. But Tauj would barter. "If you play dolls with me for thirty minutes, I'll play basketball with you for thirty minutes." How could I argue with such a plan? So more times than I wanted, I'd give in so I could have somebody to play basketball with—and you could see the outlet for my defeat on all our dolls' faces. Tauja's dolls would be organized in a line, their hair fixed just so, their outfits coordinated and pretty like princesses. Then you would find my dolls scattered around the room in various states of dress and undress, the heads off, the hair cut, some missing arms or legs. But all this was better than what eventually transpired between us on the court.

Later, Tauja would say she played basketball with me for the companionship. She played to hang out with me—and to get to play dolls with her sister. But she wound up becoming very good in the game of basketball, and I was never very good at playing dolls—especially given my tendency toward mutilating them.

While we were the best of friends, allies in a lot of ways, Tauj and I were also fiercely competitive. Maybe it began in how we tag-teamed a lot against our brother.

Poor Kenyon got the brunt of most of our conspiracies and jokes, though I was the one who got into trouble a lot because I followed Tauja. Whatever she said to do, I would do. For instance, Tauja always had money when we went to the convenience store on the corner near our house for penny candy. Yes, sometimes we'd collect coins from our piggy banks before going, but most of the time Tauj already had what we needed. Who was I to question her deep pockets? She was my spokesperson with an inexhaustible source of candy money.

Only, come to find out, the money wasn't so inexhaustible. In fact, it wasn't Tauja's. The money came from our brother's huge roll in a piggy bank he hid deep in his closet. Only no one can hide anything from Tauj.

We'd all learn, too late, that she was going into Kenyon's closet and taking change from his coin rolls. By the time he realized it, three-fourths of his piggy bank money was gone.

And I was the one who got in trouble. "I didn't know where she always got the money," I protested.

I didn't always win over my folks with my innocence. Tauja would have an idea, but because I was the curious one, I'd carry it out. So guess who got into trouble?

That's probably where our friendly competition started. Tauj could win a game of words and egg me into doing things, but on the court my actions could speak for me. For one thing, I was now growing a little faster than she was. So when we took to the driveway with the ball, just the two of us, our competition sometimes ended in a brawl. It would take Dad confiscating the ball to make us stop.

And ten minutes later Tauj and I would be the best of friends again.

4

PRESSURE

I could always see it in her eyes. She worked so
hard . . . I told her, you're gonna be great at something. Whatever you decide you want to do, you
go all the way. There's no in-between.

Harvey Catchings, former NBA player,
Philadelphia 76ers and Milwaukee Bucks

It's funny how the places that can bring you together with
someone can also be the places where you bump heads. As
much as the game of basketball brings some of my best memories of good times with my dad, it's also where we have had
our greatest struggles.

Early on, because we are such a sports family, basketball
was where Dad and I connected. Most of our time together
has been talking about basketball, watching it, playing it—
and playing the game was mostly what we did. We were

always on our way somewhere to a game: one of his or Kenyon's, or mine and Tauja's.

I see most of our similarities in basketball too. Dad always worked hard at the game and on the job. When we moved to the Chicago area, Dad became immersed in his job, going nonstop, and he involved us because his work wasn't just something he did for a paycheck. It was his passion, his life. So we'd do a lot of community outreach events as a family with the kids associated with Little City Foundation. I saw the passion Dad had for his work, and how he loved what he did so that it even spilled into what other people would call their personal time. Work was always personal for him, and it is for me too. So I believe I got a lot of my drive and work ethic from him.

Dad's bubbly, on and off the court. I remember watching him play in one game in Italy. It was Valentine's Day or Mother's Day—I don't remember the specific holiday. Mom, Kenyon, Tauj, and I were sitting on the sidelines, and all of a sudden Dad ran over to us with an armful of roses for Mom. Everyone cheered, and he handed them to her with a flourish and a kiss, then ran back to the game as everyone hooted, clapped, and cheered. He was just larger than life like that.

While I don't think of myself as larger than life, I love to do things that make people smile and bring joy, and I can be lively too, more now than when I was young and so shy.

But we're not alike at all in so many other ways. He can be hard on people. He was especially hard on me. He pushed really hard. To the point of hurt.

It didn't start that way. The turn came after seventh grade. We'd been talking about goals and what we might want to do with our lives and be when we grew up. Someone asked, "What is it you really love to do?"

My answer didn't take hours of deep thought or soul searching like some kids' did. My response was almost immediate. I wanted to play sports. While I loved volleyball, and pretty much every sport I played, there wasn't professional volleyball or professional softball at that time. Back then, even basketball didn't have a professional level for women. But that wasn't stopping me. I had every confidence that I could play in the NBA. With the guys. Just like my dad.

Claiming basketball as a profession seemed so natural. I sat down and wrote my goal on a piece of paper: "One day I'll be in the NBA."

I didn't write, "I'll be in the NBA despite the fact that I'm a girl." No, I wrote, "One day I'll be in the NBA." Period. I would follow in my father's footsteps, be like Dad playing pro, but not necessarily because of him. I was going to do it my way.

I took that paper and pinned that bad boy on my bathroom mirror, and every day when I woke up that's the first thing I saw. I looked in the mirror and saw my dream, my goal, right there, and it became more achievable, more attainable, day by day.

Of course Tauj asked about it. "What's this?"

"You know," I told her. She did know. She could always read me, but also there was my goal written in black and white and on paper for her and anyone to see on our bathroom mirror.

"Have you told Mom and Dad?"

I did then. If I didn't, I knew Tauj would. She was always good at being my confidante, but she was good at getting into all our business too. So I announced, "Mom, Dad, this is what I want to do." I didn't ask for their permission or blessing. I just knew this was what I was going to do.

To their credit, they didn't say, "Well, honey, that's nice. You can be good at basketball, but no females play in the NBA." They never once shot down my dream. I love them for that kind of encouragement for and belief in not just me but my brother and my sister too: *Whatever you want to do, we know you can do it.*

Dad seemed extra supportive. He said, "You know, if you work hard and continue to focus on what's needed, playing pro is definitely something you can do." Then he went a step further. "I'll help you as much as you want me to help you," he said.

And that's how it started.

Dad's words still echo in my head: "Tamika, as soon as you say, 'Dad, I don't want you to help,' or, 'Dad, I don't want to play basketball anymore,' or whatever the case may be, never feel like I'm going to look down on you or anything. If pro basketball is something you choose to do, and right now you want to play, great. But if you get to a point where you don't want to play anymore, then I'm behind you moving on and doing something else."

A lot of kids would think that's awesome. And I did too. Of course.

What I didn't expect was what Dad's support meant *every moment I was in the game.* His way of helping was to be in the game with me, watch every move, analyze it, bring up the missed opportunities or where I could have been stronger. His support meant to push, and he pushed too hard sometimes.

He was demanding. He was that dad who wants you to do more, be greater, shine brighter. "You're so much better," he'd say. "Your teammates are looking for you to step up your game."

"Yeah, Dad."

"You can give them so much more."

"I know, Dad."

"Your team's only going to be as successful as you are, you know. If you're not taking over the game, who do you expect to do it?"

Yeah.

He was *that dad*.

Having *that dad* was hard for me because I've always been a team player. I like to pass the ball. I like everyone to get involved. I like to see what we can do together. I never wanted to be the only one in the spotlight. I tried to tell him this once.

"That's great," he said. "But you need to score more. You need to shoot more."

What can I say? I felt like his love was conditional at times. Maybe he loved me more when I did great but not as much when I didn't do great. We bumped heads like that a lot.

Mom stayed out of it. But Tauja often defended me.

I remember one time—rather, I remember a lot of times—when Tauja had to step in and still the waters between us. Starting in high school, and more recently in my WNBA career, I never performed well when my dad was in the stands for fear that I wouldn't do enough, or I wouldn't play well enough and would have to hear his rambling about would've, could've, should've. Finally, after enough tears, arguments, and then silence between us, Tauja had a conversation with him.

"You know, Dad, sometimes you're way too hard on Mik. She loves the game so much, but sometimes you take her joy away. Sometimes she's not looking for you to be her coach. She just wants you to be her dad."

Dad responded with, "I just know she can do more. Her team is relying on her, and it's frustrating when you know someone's potential and they're not meeting it. I don't want her to be like me."

Of course, that struck a nerve with Tauj and she had to let him know. "Dad, she's already done more than you did in your career. She's her hardest critic and you just make it worse sometimes. I think you need to stop thinking about you and your career and focus on being positive to help her in her career."

I needed that bridge. As I got better and more active in the game, Dad's expectations became bigger, heavier, deeper waters to tread. Sometimes I felt so adrift from him. It wasn't so much what he was pushing me to do that felt hard; it was that he had this standard of perfection I wasn't meeting on the court, only that transferred to off the court too. I felt maybe I wasn't acceptable if I wasn't perfect. I wasn't fitting into his picture of me as a daughter, the basketball star. It was that unbearable weight of trying to fit in again, only this time in my own family, with my own dad.

That weight plunges deep into you, hurts deeper than I can say.

I never felt that kind of judgment from Mom. Whether or not I played well, she always met me after a game and said, "Oh, Tamika—you played great." Even when I didn't play great, she'd say that same thing.

Sometimes I'd call her on it. "Mom, no, I wasn't my best tonight. I didn't play great."

"It doesn't matter," she said. "You're my daughter. I'm so proud of you out there. I loved how you played and put your heart into it. I love you just the way you are."

She reminded me how trying, keeping on, even when the odds are against you, is what counts. I never felt like she disapproved of me or that I wasn't measuring up or wasn't qualified for the game if I wasn't my best—or, worse, messed up—one night.

It's such a huge gift to have someone tell you, *I see you as you are. I see you as you can be. I know you are getting better every day. Even if you're not better now, I love you anyway.*

Anyway closes a lot of gaps that can separate people.

I wish Dad could have understood that. I wish he could have seen how important it is to say, "I think you're great anyway," or, "You did great tonight and will do even better tomorrow."

Now I think he maybe just applied the same standard to me that he did to himself—and that he'd tried to put on Kenyon and Tauj before me.

Kenyon got that weight first. He played basketball really well and was an All-American. By his junior year in high school he already had a number of scholarship offers. Then, before his senior year, he was really ill. He had incredible pain, lost weight, couldn't eat. He went through a series of tests, and just before his senior year in high school he was diagnosed with Crohn's disease, a chronic inflammatory condition of the gastrointestinal tract. He couldn't play. He lost all the athletic scholarships, but he got an academic scholarship because he's so smart and worked so hard to

45

learn and excel in school, one of so many reasons I've always admired him and wanted to be like him. All Dad's pressure on Kenyon turned to Tauja because she was so good at basketball too. Only she didn't really want to hear his criticisms and analysis, his pointers and all those pushes. She played because she was good at it. She saw how you could get a scholarship for what you were good at, and so she kept playing, but basketball wasn't her thing. Besides, she and Dad had a different relationship from mine and Dad's. I was the youngest. And in the end, Dad's wishes and expectations for at least one of his kids to excel in basketball fell on me. And I felt the pressure.

But the difference was that I had the passion for basketball. And I felt it was *my* game. Not Dad's.

For a lot of years, I didn't know how to get Dad to hear me. His "coaching" just made me feel, once again, like I didn't fit in, that I wasn't acceptable. I felt silenced. For a long time, I just took it all in and stuffed it, all the hurt and frustration and confusion about how to get him to see I could play the game well my own way.

I journaled a lot during those years.

Once, in high school, I did sit down with Dad to talk about his expectations. I wasn't sure where to start, so I cut right to the point. "You want too much. You expect perfection. You're putting too much pressure on me. It's as if you're living through me and it's not fair."

He didn't hear me. To him, this was another opportunity to say, "I see so much potential in you—why don't you see what I see? These are the things I want for you."

I wanted to say, "Yeah, but I'm living my life, not yours. The things you want for me are the things I want. The standards you want me to achieve, I want to achieve. Getting to that goal of excellence may take me a little bit longer, but this is my road and my journey, not your road and your journey. Can you see that I love what I do, but you're taking away that love by putting more expectation on me than there needs to be?"

Only I didn't say any of that to him then.

I never talked back to my dad. And even if I could have said what was in my heart and soul, for whatever reason I don't think he could have heard it. Maybe because he had such high hopes, such intense desire for me, and each of his children, to succeed in the game he loved.

That didn't change how all those hopes, all that desire for something good for others, made life so hard for me.

Part 2

NOISE

I hear it . . . the noise.
Like a drill through my mind.
It's loud, demanding, pressuring and unwanted.
It's constricting me.
Surrounding me.
Squeezing me.

To hear or not to hear?
The voices, the shame, the names.
I've come to conclude,
Sometimes silence is better than noise . . .

Noise IS a loudness to the reality of what I don't want to hear.

5

SPLIT

What I saw was a really, really quick, rather thin, high jumping young lady who didn't play the kind of defense she does now. By the time she was in eighth grade, though, she had filled out. I'd see her sitting in the stands holding a basketball and watching Tauja play as a freshman on the varsity, and it was then I thought to myself how good we could be with her on the floor.

Frank Mattucci, coach, Stevenson
High School Patriots

I hoped the move to Chicago would change my life for the better. It didn't.

School was still hard. I was still different from others, only now I was significantly taller than most of the kids my age. I was still self-conscious of how I talked (when I talked at

51

all). I still struggled to hear my own voice, let alone others'. I was still asking *huh?* A lot.

The big box hearing aids were never replaced. But I learned that wasn't what really set me apart anyway.

My problems at school weren't the worst of what was going on. Dad was gone a lot now—more than ever before. His new job was consuming his time and attention.

It wasn't going so well between Mom and Dad. I don't know if it was the move, or Dad's absences, or something else, but they were fighting a lot. And we kids were caught in the cross fire.

Tauja tended to side with Dad. I found more comfort with Mom and tended to drift toward her during this time. Kenyon . . . I don't know. He was caught in between.

I didn't want to take sides. I wanted us all to be together. I wanted to be a team player, even in the family. So when Mom and Tauj would argue, I would try to stay out of it. Most of the time, I looked for a chance to get away from it all.

The court became my sanctuary. When I had discovered basketball was my language, it also became my outlet for all the emotions, anything going on in my life. When I was happy, I'd play basketball. When I was sad, I'd play basketball. When I was frustrated or mad or overwhelmed, I'd play basketball.

Not long after we'd moved to Deerfield, the kids in the neighborhood knew this too. Beginning in fourth grade and throughout high school, guys would call our house for me.

Mom would answer the phone. She'd hear, "Is Tamika going to the court? Is she already at the court?"

Mom would turn to me, eyebrows raised. "Wait a minute," she'd say. "You're too young for this to be going on!"

But it was all about the game. The guys were my friends. Basketball friends. I didn't have any girlfriends, just guy friends—and Kenyon and Tauj.

Nothing started on the courts till I got there. All the neighborhood guys would be waiting for me. We'd pick our teams and we'd play. They all wanted me on their teams. We'd play all day if we could. If Mom couldn't find me around the house, she knew I was at the court. She would bring lunch and I'd take a break. We'd sit there and eat, talk, joke around, and then we'd go back to the game.

The game was my life, the way life was supposed to be.

Sunday nights, Dad would go to Deerfield High School for pickup games with some guys he knew. He took us kids with him. He'd get us there early so he could teach us stuff and so we could play against him. But his other friends would eventually show up, and they'd play their game while we watched. That would always upset me because I thought I should be able to play with them. I felt, at the age of ten, that I could maybe hold my own against them.

The tension between Mom and Dad got worse. They were becoming torn apart from each other and from the family.

Of course, we were torn with them. For a family that had been so close, this was devastating. Kenyon, Tauj, and I had done everything together. We felt tension too. We started to take sides. There wasn't just an *us* anymore. There was now a *her* and *him* and *us*.

Tauja and Mom clashed more and more on little things that turned into big things. I tried not to let that become a rift between Tauj and me, but sometimes we couldn't avoid it. She became critical of Mom. I tended to be critical of Dad. Some things we couldn't talk about now.

Kenyon, the oldest, probably was affected the most by our parents' tension. He was heading into ninth grade and trying to find himself in his own way. Moving so many times in so many years hadn't helped. Still, he seemed to keep his head on straight, finding a balance and some inner quiet. I believe basketball may have been his sanctuary too.

By the time I started sixth grade, Mom and Dad had divorced.

Dad moved down the street—not far, but emotionally it felt to us like he was back in Italy. It felt odd for Dad to be in another house. It wasn't right.

I had all these emotions and preteen hormones going on, and the one place I knew I could deal with it all was on the court, facing the hoop, running the lines. Basketball was the one thing that would never let me down. It was the thing I loved that loved me back.

Of course my parents loved me. Of course I loved them and Tauja and Kenyon. But our relationships got tricky for us during these years. Sometimes we had to work out whose side we were on in this issue or that. With basketball, rules were the rules. I knew them and there were no questions. I could play the game and know everything would always be okay.

There's playing basketball and there's the *game* of basketball. I began to love the *game* of basketball even more during this time. Some people say they "love" a particular sport, but really they're just saying they have fun playing it. And most people can say that.

No, you really fall in love with a game when you begin to appreciate what it does for you inside.

I'd go to the gym or the court earlier, stay later, spend time when no one else was around. It was a zone I could enter to be at peace. I realized peace came especially when I was the first one on the court. I treasured being the first one at the gym, walking into the silence. That may sound funny coming from someone who struggled to hear, but there is a silence when you're alone on the court unlike any other. You don't have to worry about anyone screaming or yelling, the murmur of others on the sidelines, or music or crowds abuzz.

Alone on the court, there's no background noise as there is in life. There are just basketball sounds. The rhythm of the ball on the court or against the backboard, the whoosh through the hoop, that squeak of your tennis shoes on the waxed wood. I love the sound of tennies squeaking as they work the court. The music of the game.

In basketball, I kept growing and becoming better. The game wouldn't keep me in a box, make me always be what I had been in the past. I could change and try new things without repercussion. I could play just myself, or for my team when it was all about *us* doing and being our best. Even when we played a *them*, the lines were so clear. It wasn't confusing as it was within my own family. I didn't have to think about anyone being hurt. I just played the game and the rules were the rules and I did what I did and that was it.

By seventh grade, my love for the game was unequivocal. I knew basketball was what I wanted to work at. Forever. I'm so glad I had found that clarity because life got even more confusing with family.

Tauja, more at odds with Mom than ever, moved in with Dad.

That was a jolt. We'd shared the same space, language, everything. We'd been inseparable. I was her sidekick. She was the one who spoke for me; the instigator who drew us into trouble, yes, but she also gave me a certain confidence and courage. And she was that bridge between Dad and me. She could speak her mind, and if you didn't like what she said, so be it. She was that one. I thought about things more, brooded over them.

So when Tauja went to live with Dad, even though she was just down the street, it made me really sad.

I knew she would still be my protective sister, even if she wasn't under the same roof with me. And she was. Whenever my feelings would get hurt by something Dad said or hard times we'd go through, him being so hard on me, Tauj would stick up for me. So we were still "together," Tauj and I, but it was a different together. Dad's distance we'd gotten used to. I would never get used to being apart from Tauja.

My inner circle, or little family, was what I still clung to, even when we were in this position of having to take sides and decide where to live. Dad living down the street, and Tauj no longer in the bedroom next to mine—I wasn't okay with any of it. It wasn't right.

Tauja and I coped with it as best we could. We saw each other every day at school and talked together before and after. And at one point we wound up playing on the same team.

My life began to change. I had my goal—"One day I'll be in the NBA"—pinned to my bathroom mirror, and I began to work toward it. School was always important to me, and even with my hearing struggles I kept up a B+ average. And in basketball I was now striving not just to play the game but to work at the game.

Every day I'd get up, get dressed, watch some basketball on TV (there was always a game on some channel), and then go to school, only to look for breaks when I could go to the court, practice, and play with friends. Most were older, bigger guys I'd meet on the court. They'd wait for me every day. We'd egg each other on—I wanted to show them I could be just as good and even better than they were. We'd play hard. And I would hustle, scrambling for every loose ball. At times bikes were lined up on one side of the court, and when the ball would bounce into that row of bikes, I wouldn't hesitate to dive after it.

I was competitive in my schoolwork too. I always did my homework right after school. And basketball became another kind of homework. If I wasn't at an official team practice or playing other sports—volleyball and softball during their seasons—I was outside shooting hoops. That was my routine. Every day.

Even during the summer, I was up at seven or seven thirty in the morning and rushed through breakfast so I could get to the court. I loved it when Kenyon and Tauja were there. We could play together, the Catchingses, like old times. But even without them, I turned to the court.

The game got me through.

When Tauja became a freshman, she made the varsity basketball team at Stevenson High School.

As an eighth-grader, I'd go over to the high school to watch her practice. I'd sit in the stands, holding a basketball, and literally itch to get out there and play. I'd rub my arm and then bounce the ball and think of the times Tauj and I went against one another in the driveway at home; how different it would be to pass the ball to her, or to grab it from a toss from her and work together to win. And because I knew I was an even match with Tauja in the driveway, I could imagine myself fitting in on a varsity basketball team, playing successfully against juniors and seniors.

That wouldn't happen yet, but it was something I looked forward to in another year.

Watching her on that Stevenson court, I saw what an incredible player Tauja was—naturally gifted, graceful, elegant. She could run fast and fluid, like she was sailing. She was incredible at defense. Where I worked harder to be faster, score, make the shots from far away or up close, and do what it took to rebound, Tauj was a great defensive player, especially when she played a full-court press, disrupting the opposing player's dribble and often forcing a turnover.

I learned a lot from watching her. And I learned quickly. When we had played before, we were just playing one-on-one, with the emphasis on scoring. Now I was driven and intentional about how to step up my game defensively. I paid attention to how people played, how the team worked together, how I was performing around other players. And I learned that playing tougher defense and forcing turnovers was as noteworthy and valuable as sinking a basket.

Any excitement I felt about basketball—the player I was becoming and the potential that lay ahead—was tempered by tough times at home. And while Tauja and I were close even after she got into high school and was playing on the varsity team, we also had some rough patches.

But I had to let all that go. There was going to be sadness, distance, and frustration. There would be some jealousy, some resentment. It was going to be that way at times. It wasn't going to be the same as before. But that was okay. There was always basketball.

The game would always get me through.

In 1993, now a freshman, I made the varsity basketball team at Stevenson High School. We weren't just Tauja and Tamika anymore. We became "the Catchings Sisters." Together, the two of us got good, really good. Kids, teachers, and coaches all started noticing us. We started to wear that identity together, and we became popular for what we did on the court.

Tauja and I—"the Catchings Sisters"—were playing together on the same team, on the court in IHSAA games that really meant something.

I had grown, and at six feet I was now an inch taller than Tauja. The Stevenson coach, Frank Mattucci, played Tauja at forward and me at center, but our play was an up-tempo offense where Tauja and I often raced up both sides of the court, feeding the ball to whomever was left most open. Our chemistry—as girls who had played so much together in the driveway as well as sisters who were so close as to almost read each other's minds—became evident right away on the court. In November, the two of us scored forty points in a game against York High School.

One of the things we became known for—and that became a hallmark of the Stevenson teams to come—was our trapping defense. As an opposing player would bring the ball up the court, Tauja would come up to her in the backcourt, spread her long arms out, and force the player toward the sideline. Meanwhile, I would slide over quickly, taking advantage of the fact that Tauja was in the other player's line of vision. As the opposing player tried to dribble out of the trap, she'd turn into me on her blind side. We became remarkably effective at forcing turnovers.

On and off the court, we were now one another's sidekick, and I valued that deeply. We'd been like twins ever since I could remember. Tauja not only spoke for me but she really could read my thoughts. She could sense like no one else how I was feeling at any given moment—if I was frustrated or what I found funny, what troubled me or made me purely happy.

At the same time, something inside me yearned to be just me, Tamika, not "a Catchings Sister." While I wanted the connection with Tauja, I also wanted to be myself, seen for my own abilities and valued for who I was personally. It was just the seedling of an inner conflict that would grow in the next two years—on the one hand cherishing the sister partnership we had, but on the other hand desiring my own independence.

Meanwhile, what Tauja and I were doing on the court, together, was becoming really special.

"There go the Catchings Sisters!"

I opened my eyes wide toward Tauja, and we stepped it up to get to the checkout counter before more people noticed us and started talking. I hoped we could duck out before anyone followed us.

For me, these sightings were now overwhelming. At the mall, the grocery store, the movie theater, in the hallways at school—pretty much everywhere we went—more and more strangers recognized us from our games and the newspapers. The buzz was about such equally matched sisters, so close in age, just twenty-one months apart, "taking over the court," as one reporter said. "Star basketball sisters." "The Sister Act." "Daughters of an NBA father." The headlines kept on coming. "The Catchings sisters are to basketball what the Williams sisters, Venus and Serena, are to tennis," the media reported. "Champions." "Competitors and rivals but blood and best friends." "A powerhouse together and just as strong apart."

A trip to the mall was no longer just a trip to the mall. Other kids, parents, and adults, most strangers to us, stared and called us by name. Sometimes they followed us or rushed forward asking for autographs. They took pictures and wanted to talk, shake our hands, give us hugs. We couldn't go anywhere without getting noticed.

The shy girl in me was getting called out, and it was hard. Not the same kind of hard as with the put-downs and bullying in grade school, but still unnerving. How do you tell people who mean well with their compliments and admiration that you just want to be treated like everyone else? How do you turn away from anyone excited to meet you?

Tauj didn't seem as troubled with our celebrity as I was. She loved meeting new people and thrived in the spotlight. In college Tauja would take a job as a customer service rep for a mortuary. No joke. And she was good at it, selling burial plots to people while they were eating dinner. She was always caring, and outgoing and genuine in zeroing in on what you needed. She could engage anyone in conversation about anything, sell coffins to the living. People loved her.

I leaned on that magnetism, and it was called out a little more every day. A lot of our high school games were televised. Photos of us appeared everywhere. There was footage of Tauj flying down the court like a gazelle and of me shooting from the outside or laying the ball up on the glass.

Coaches, our own and the ones on opposing teams, were constantly remarking on us as sister players. Everyone commented how we were a package deal, the Sister Act of the game.

Our coach, Frank Mattucci, handled our celebrity well, and he was careful not to give either of us reasons to resent the other. Rather than compare us, Coach Mattucci praised both Tauj and me for our strengths. He pushed us equally on what we could work on to improve. He said comparing us would be like comparing a Monet with a da Vinci. Can't each be remarkable in her own way?

I liked that. He put in words what I'd been feeling for a long time, both on the court and in the classroom—in life, really. We are each gifted in a special way. God made us with some aspect of his own image, and we are, in our own unique way, God's work of art.

Reporters, of course, remained fascinated with the differences between Tauj and me. They began to come to practices, seek us out before and after games. I'd stand behind Tauj or to the side and just smile. I had a hard time hearing and even more difficult time speaking. My self-consciousness had only grown without the hearing aids or the speech therapy. Besides, Tauj could talk her way into and out of anything, and I was fine with her speaking for me.

As much as I was pushing myself during this time, it was a golden period. I was coming into my own, even in playing alongside Tauj. I was just fifteen years old, not able to drive a car yet, but really good at driving a ball. More determined than ever, I knew I could be better, and I embraced that, relishing the challenge ahead.

Coach Mattucci knew he had something special going into the 1994–1995 season. Besides Tauja and me, he had Katie Coleman, a sharp-shooting guard who could drill threes. But Coach Mattucci had another secret weapon—himself.

He had coached Class A ball with Luther North, and in four years had compiled an astonishing 102–14 record. In 1990 he came to Class AA Stevenson, which had had a struggling program. His philosophy was sometimes called "the Mattucci Way"—an emphasis on tough, relentless, stifling defense, and within a few years it was paying off.

In my sophomore year, Stevenson would go 32–2, making its way easily through the postseason contests to the state finals.

In the championship game, we would play a strong team from Chicago, Mother McCauley, which had achieved a lot in the first year of a new coach. They had strength on the inside with a big strong center, but we felt we could do some damage with our speed.

And with our defense. We came out playing a full-court press—Coach Mattucci's strategy to take a quick advantage in the game. And it worked. We forced turnover after turnover, scoring most times we had the ball. At one point several minutes into the game, Mother McCauley had not yet even taken a shot. By the five-minute mark, we led 10–0.

On one play, I had been fouled, made my free throws, and one of the Mother McCauley players was taking the ball up the court. Tauja was defending to one side and edged around to the player's left. Seeing that, I raced from front court on the opponent's other side. The player, seeing me, turned the other way and ran into Tauja, who slapped the ball away and took possession. It was the Mattucci Way, stifling defense. It was also the Catchings Sisters Way, an intuitive sense of the game from years of playing each other on our driveway. It was a beautiful thing.

That championship game became a physical game, a lot of scrapping for the ball, elbows flying, some hard bumps bruises, and blood. Katie Coleman went down for a time with a severe blow to her head. Mother McCauley climbed back into the game when we relaxed our full-court press.

I got into early foul trouble, and Coach kept me on the bench for part of the second quarter. But Tauja played great in my absence, at one point scoring a tough layup inside while getting fouled. She sank her free throw, then raced down to the other end to defend an opponent racing in for a basket. Tauja got there first, planted her feet, and took the charge.

Stevenson weathered the comeback, and we started building our lead again. At the half we were up by eighteen points, within sight of Stevenson's first girls' basketball championship.

During halftime, selections to the All-State team were announced. It is one of the highest honors in high school sports. Both Tauja and I were chosen and accepted our awards on the court. The Catchings Sisters were considered the best in girls' high school basketball that year.

The second half was never close. We would win by thirty points, which I think was the greatest point spread for a championship ever. When the final buzzer went off, Tauja and I screamed, jumped up, and embraced each other. I had done well, scoring twelve points, despite foul trouble early. Tauja excelled, scoring eighteen points, the high scorer for the team. And it was our tandem defense that had set the tone for the game and helped Stevenson jump out to a big lead.

The Catchings Sisters, in just our sophomore and junior years in high school, had made even bigger headlines. But there was one headline coming that Tauja and I didn't expect.

The award for the best female player in Illinois high school basketball is called Ms. Basketball of Illinois. It's an award given by a ballot of coaches and media throughout the state. The award is made several weeks after the high school championship game.

Any number of players could rightly have been so honored, not the least of which was Tauja.

Instead the award was given to me. I never expected it. For one thing, they don't give it to underclassmen. They had never given it to a sophomore before.

In writing about the award that year, a *Chicago Tribune* reporter said, "What strikes you most about The Kid—after you have witnessed her cool demeanor, have been awed by her abundance of God-given talent and watched her stop defenders in their tracks, dart up the floor and soar toward the basket like a hoop-seeking missile—is her age. What strikes you most—after you have certified her NBA bloodlines and charted her limitless future—is that she is still only 15 years old. 15. Too young to drive. But not too young, the record shows, to drive her opponents to distraction. Old enough to lead a team, the record shows, but not too old to act like a kid."[1]

What the writer had right was that I was still a kid. I was a six-foot, fifteen-year-old who could play basketball. But I still struggled publicly with all this celebrity. I was asked how I was handling this award and the attention I was getting. "It's difficult," I said, "when people come up to you—people you don't even know—and congratulate you. Everybody wants to be your friend. My sister, Tauja, and I and a friend were at the mall one day when two guys walked up to us and said, 'Wow! Aren't you the Catchings Sisters?' Sometimes I sit in bed at night and wish I could go somewhere where nobody knows me. People are always treating me like I'm someone special."

I was also afraid of the world out there without Tauja standing in front of me. But lying in bed the night of the Ms. Basketball of Illinois award, I was grateful for my opportunities at such a young age, happy to see what I could achieve. In a way, I wanted to be Tamika and not "one of the Catchings Sisters." I wanted so much more from basketball, and I wasn't sure Tauja wanted that for herself. I wanted to go pro, and that still seemed a long way away. But I was willing to work for it. The court was my life, where I came alive inside.

So I prayed this was only the beginning.

The next morning I got up and glanced at the Ms. Basketball of Illinois trophy, but then quickly fixed my eyes on that scrap of paper on the mirror, my goal written in my seventh-grade penmanship: "One day I'll be in the NBA."

I put on my sweats, grabbed my basketball, and headed to the gym.

6

TEXAS

A lot of our kids had played together for many years, from junior high and now in high school. When Tamika walked out onto the court, they had to acclimate themselves to playing with someone who could do things they weren't ready for. They had to learn to play up to her level—her power, her strength, her quickness—and her ability to make a pass that you might not be expecting.

Sara Hackerott, head coach, Duncanville
High School girls' basketball, 1993–1998

"This is the worst decision I've ever made. I can't do this." I was in tears and inconsolable the night before starting another new school, in another new town.

I'd moved back to Texas—with Mom and without Tauja— and I felt utterly alone. I was the one who decided to make the move, and Mom, after plenty of "are you sure" questions, packed up our stuff and we headed to Texas.

But now I faced another new school, and this time truly on my own, without Tauja by my side as interpreter, defender, protector, and sometimes peacemaker, my very ears and voice much of the time. The memories of all those "firsts" in Abilene years before came crawling back: the first time meeting new kids, the first time they saw me as different, the first time being called out for not fitting in. You never really escape the weight of those firsts.

I began to feel paralyzed with fear. It had been a while since I'd felt overcome like this. I'd worked so hard in Deerfield to find my place at school and discover the language where I was fluent—on the court, working out and practicing till I earned the other kids' and people's respect.

Now I was back to the same old challenges, the same old feelings.

Poor Mom. I really put her through it. "I can't believe you brought me here," I cried at one point. "I hate you for making me move."

I didn't hate her and she knew it. And, of course, she never made me move with her. I was just so done-in that night. She kept trying to comfort me. She reminded me I'd chosen this. She knew I would get through. She believed in me.

But that night before I started my junior year in Duncanville, Texas, she had one distraught daughter and faced as much of an unknown as I did about how we were going to make this work.

For her, it was about putting the disappointment and losses of divorce behind her. She had a lot of support in Texas, all her family—my grandparents, aunts and uncles, cousins.

You need people who love you to be by your side, not just figuratively but physically, when you're starting something new. It's like their presence, their touch, gives you courage and strength.

Kenyon had just started college at Northern Illinois University. Tauja would be starting college in another year and was living with Dad. So Mom felt the timing was right for her to start a new life of her own.

Her decision was a life-changer for all of us. Since the divorce, Kenyon, Tauja, and I had found our own ways of maintaining our connection as a family. While we had no longer been under the same roof every night, we had been together during the day at school. We had eaten lunches together, hung out, played together on the same basketball and other sports teams, and talked on the phone every day. We were living just minutes apart, and when we needed to meet up, we could. We fought to stay close as siblings.

But that same closeness that had helped us kids get through those years, especially Tauj and me, may have been the thing that was so hard for Mom. For her, living separate and yet so close was the constant reminder of a family that was broken and a marriage that had failed. For Mom, moving to Texas was a way of putting all of that behind her, making it just a distant memory in the rearview mirror.

But for me, being umpteen miles from Tauja created a huge empty space inside. *Those 960 miles might as well be 960 million*, I thought that night before beginning my junior year in Duncanville.

I picked up the phone that night and called Tauj. "I can't believe I'm starting school without you," I cried.

"I know. Me too," she said.

We cried together for a long time.

My decision to make the move with Mom was my own, but it was one I made after a lot of discussion with Tauja.

In hallmark style, she was quick to speak out about what she was going to do. This was her senior year of high school. She didn't want to miss that, finishing with all the kids she'd gone through school with the longest. She didn't want to move back to Texas.

I got that. Graduating with your high school friends was a big deal.

More privately I thought, *Tauj and Mom still butt heads a lot. It will be tough on all of us if they keep fighting a lot.*

As for me, I wanted to stay with Mom. The more I excelled in basketball, the more Dad's expectations were in high gear, and the struggles in our relationship were at their height. Besides, I couldn't bear to think of Mom being all alone.

Always that team player part of me, even at home, you know?

There was another thing. I had, quite frankly, been growing tired of "the Catchings Sisters" circus constantly surrounding us. I wondered what it would be like to play without Tauj, not part of a "Dynamic Duo," or "Powerhouse Sisters," or any of the other media-clever names they called us.

The idea of going solo was not directed at Tauja. Maybe it reflected my own inner sense of destiny. *My* destiny. Maybe it reflected what I knew: that for Tauja basketball was *a* thing, not *the* thing. For me it was *the* thing. The *only* thing. And I wasn't sure how I could be all I could be playing basketball if I were to most people simply a Catchings sister. The younger one.

If I moved to Duncanville, maybe I could see just how good I was or could be. I thought, *I'm ready to be on my own, to be wholly, completely Tamika Catchings, not just a part of the Catchings Sisters.* So, I reasoned, the move could be good. Duncanville wouldn't be like Abilene. I'd have cousins and aunts and uncles around, more support. I knew them. We'd made trips from Illinois back to Texas for Christmas all these years. And I knew my place now. I knew I could get respect on the court.

I wanted to be, needed to be, just Tamika.

On the practical side, I was halfway through high school. I reasoned that I would have two years to make my mark, whether I stayed in Illinois or went to Texas, and one of those years I'd be playing without Tauja anyway. She was going to go off to college.

And so I had decided. I would move to Texas with Mom.

In that decision, Tauj and I made a pact. We'd find a way to play together in college. This separation would be just a couple of years, then we'd be back together. It would be okay.

My decision was announced to my school and then the press. The Chicago newspaper headline, one that many never expected, read, "Illinois Ms. Basketball Taking Her Trophy to Texas."

"Tamika, you're going to go through this like you always do," Mom told me that night I was in a fit of tears. "How can you know you won't like this school? You haven't even been there a day yet. Give it a try. If you don't like it here, you can always go back to Deerfield and live with your dad."

In all my reasoning about making the move, I hadn't thought long enough about how much I needed Tauj by my side, not only in the game but after and in practices when reporters wanted interviews or strangers wanted to meet me. I'd relied on her for so long. I'd always looked around for her in difficult or new situations to speak for me, to be my ears. I don't think I realized till that night before starting school in Duncanville just how silent I'd stayed around the court and in school for those first sixteen years of my life.

Oh, God, I prayed. *I chose this. It was my doing. Somehow,* I asked God, *get me through.* It was an exercise in faith, which you can't really have in the presence of doubt. But my faith was wobbly. So was the courage I'd briefly found in deciding to move—every bit seemed to spill out of me with all those tears.

The next morning, with eyes still puffy from crying the night before, I walked into Duncanville High School and prepared for the worst. I realized how alone I was.

And yet, quickly, I wasn't alone. Being new was okay.

Those weeks before school I'd made my way to the open gym and the outdoor courts in the surrounding neighborhood. The guys there noticed my skills.

"You're good," one of them said.

With that, we started playing. He and his buddies welcomed me, and in the days following they looked for me. I'd go back to the gym or the court, and the same guys would be there, and we'd divide into teams and play. It was so much easier for me to meet people on the court. I didn't have to talk a lot. I relied on the language of the game. So in those few weeks before school I got to know some kids, enough that one of the guys, a boy named Sam, decided to give me a nickname.

"We're going to call you *Shaq*fu" he said. Some kind of twist on Shaquille O'Neal's name.

"Shaqfu?" Even if I hadn't had trouble hearing, I would have checked what he was saying.

"Yeah," Sam said. "Shaqfu because you're so much taller than everybody, and because you're going to stomp on any of the girls, even the best."

"Because you're *good*," another guy said. "Because you dominate the game."

Shaqfu? I gave Sam and his buddies the eye. "Yeah, that's not my name," I said, but deep down, liking that nickname or not, I knew I was in. I had respect from some kids already.

Once again, basketball would get me through.

And so I discovered that first day at Duncanville High School that the respect was waiting for me.

The guys I'd met on the court were welcoming. They acknowledged me in the hallway. They called me by that nickname, which I didn't really like but knew was a term of endearment and acceptance. It wasn't like other names I'd been called and dreaded through that long night before.

I was still the new girl, still wasn't sure if I would belong here. But I wasn't called out for not fitting in. Rather, I was standing out for being special. Standing out suddenly wasn't so bad.

For the first time, being new and special was a way to connect. Kids would check on me. "Oh, you're new. Do you need anything? Finding your way around all right?"

It was refreshing. There was kindness. This wasn't a re-play of Abilene. I had proven myself, and my reputation had followed me. And I was discovering that I had changed. For all my shyness still, I was a little more outgoing and more comfortable around people than when I was younger. I had learned some things watching Tauja around people. In a way, because of that, she was still with me.

And God was there, answering my prayers. I realized that, in fact, it wasn't basketball that got me through.

When I was growing up, we regularly went to church. It was important to my parents and it was what we did as a family. I'm not sure it was important to me so much. Like a lot of kids, I guess, I didn't think a lot about God in a personal way. Church was a place I should go on Sundays, and it reinforced for me as a kid what was right and wrong. I remember being involved in Children's Church, Teen Ministry, Kids of the Kingdom, Vacation Bible School, and in whatever else our parents wanted us to participate at different times in my life. Church put the Bible in my life in the form of Bible stories. That was good, but I don't think I ever met God in a personal way.

When we moved to Duncanville, Mom and I went to Oak Cliff Bible Fellowship, a church pastored by Tony Evans. I started to experience God in a different way. I'm not saying my faith became all it should be. But I found a sense of faith something more connected to life than it had been for me before that. It could have been getting older, or simply opening up to receive the Word. Dr. Evans taught the Bible in a way that met me right where I was, or in whatever situation I was dealing with. His teachings gave me a sense of purpose and an understanding of how God had given me all the gifts I possessed. I experienced a true awakening moment to what it meant to be a Christian.

During that time I also developed a keen interest in Christian music. Preachers tell you what you put into your mind and into your body has a direct effect on you. While you may hear me listening to Christian or country or something else, I like music that has a good message and sometimes just a good beat to nod your head to. That's the power of music.

Interestingly, one of the cheerleaders at Duncanville High School was Anthony Evans, Tony Evans's son. We became friends, and we've kept in touch through the years. Of course, he's gone on to become a stellar Christian music artist and has even performed on *The Voice*.

In the next days and weeks, I tried out for sports, made both the volleyball and basketball teams, and started getting to know the players. We ate lunch together, met up after class, and hung out after school and on weekends. I didn't have Tauj and it wasn't the same, but it was all right. I was doing okay.

Duncanville High School had strong sports programs. They'd won titles in soccer, baseball, and basketball, including a number of titles in girls' basketball. Duncanville took its basketball program seriously. However, in recent years there had been a drought. The girls' basketball team hadn't won a championship since 1990.

Our volleyball team was led by Coach Jan Briggs, who was a veteran volleyball coach and had had a very successful career. Under her leadership that year, our volleyball team won the state championship.

My success on the volleyball court didn't hurt my early standing with the other kids in high school. But I was beginning to realize that the kids, while being impressed with my athletic ability, actually liked me for who I was. I relaxed some, and found myself with some good friends to hang out with.

The year before I got there, the Duncanville girls' basketball team had made it to the state finals. It was a good team, but they lost the title game to Austin Westlake in overtime. Three starters, however, returned the next year, when I got there. They had strong talent. What they lacked was a center.

My new coach, Sara Hackerott, had started coaching the team in 1993–1994, taking over for a legend, Sandra Meadows, who led the Duncanville Pantherettes during the late eighties. At one point her teams compiled a consecutive winning streak of 134 games. Coach Meadows had contracted cancer, later passing away in 1994. Now Coach Hackerott, once Meadows's assistant coach, was making her own mark, determined for the team to overcome its disappointment the year before.

She says she didn't really know what she was getting when I walked onto the court at Duncanville. She'd heard some things about me, but kids come and go, she would say, and all kinds of talk precedes those who transfer in. "You never know how much of the reputation you hear is real, and what a girl can actually do on the court," she says.

Coach Hackerott tells a story about me. One afternoon in October, a few of the girls on the team were in the gym hanging out, some practicing certain shots and moves. Her back was to the court as she was doing some paperwork. At one point she heard a rim rattle. Her head popped up. As she tells it, she was surprised to hear that sound—it was only heard when the guys played, guys who could jump so high as to pull down on the rim. There were no guys in the gym.

Coach Hackerott turned around and saw me. "What did you just do, Tamika?" she asked.

I looked at her sheepishly, with a slight smile.

"Whatever it was, I want you to back up and do it again," she said.

I just looked at her. I didn't say anything. Then I took a few steps back to the free throw line, took several quick running leaps toward the basket, jumped high, and batted the rim.

The rim rattled once again.

Coach Hackerott smiled. Later she would say that put a punctuation mark on what she'd heard about me. It was then she really knew what I could do on the court.

Of course, I'd played center back at Stevenson. Coaches in high school didn't know quite how to play me—at the time, I was taller than many other high school players, so I was often used at center. Growing up, I'd developed moves like a forward, and I knew how to back into the basket against a defender, then move fast enough to swing one way or the other for a close shot. I often brought the ball up the court, like a point guard. Some referred to me as a "point center."

At Duncanville, I was often used at center and filled a hole they had in their starting five. We did well that year, finishing the regular season with a 29–2 record.

As we entered the playoffs, we were ranked second in the state of Texas and fifteenth in the nation.

Meanwhile, back in Chicago, Tauja and the Stevenson Patriots had finished 34–1 and were entering their playoffs as the favored team, likely to repeat our championship run the year before.

Of course, there was media interest in the two of us, now on different teams, both vying for titles in different states. Dad would be interviewed about that and would suggest that we both could win state championships that year. Dad's comments could be interpreted as pride or as pressure. Sometimes I wasn't sure how to take them.

Duncanville didn't make it through even the areas (quarterfinals), disappointing everyone. Stevenson stayed strong and tore through teams, while Tauja was relentless on both ends of the court—proving that she had just as much skill as I did. As Tauja led the Patriots to the championship round, Mom and I flew up to Chicago to surprise her.

She was shooting around right before the game and I was positioned up in the stands behind the backboard. After one of her shots floated to the basket, she looked up and saw me. Our eyes connected and she flew off the court up into the stands.

"Surprise!!!" I screamed.

What a happy moment! We exchanged a few words, and then she flew back down to the court, looking back to make sure I was really there. I was so proud of my big sis. Tauja led Stevenson to its second straight state title and we all celebrated as if I were still there. I was truly happy for Tauja and for Stevenson. And while I was disappointed that Duncanville didn't do better in the playoffs, I was happy for the move I'd chosen to make and the year that was. And secretly, I was relieved that Tauja and I didn't wind up in some cheesy headline about us both winning state championships.

I had left the Catchings Sisters act far behind.

In basketball, there's always a tension between playing as a team and asserting yourself as the go-to player. It was never my style to assert myself that way, and it still isn't, but it became more of an issue when I got to Duncanville.

No one player, no matter how talented, can be so good as to take over a game single-handedly. One person can't beat five opposing players on her own. And when one player begins to take over a game, her teammates usually start to stand around and watch. If you're not careful, you can take the rest of your teammates out of the game.

I'd always thought of myself as a team player, and that's how I enjoyed playing the game—passing off the ball to the open shooter, running plays, drawing players to defend me, then dropping the ball off to my teammate who was streaking to the basket. That's what good basketball is all about. And I think at Duncanville, all my instincts for team play became even more developed. But there was a point when I needed to play differently.

I was still just a kid, but I was aware that others on our team were looking at me as playing on a higher level. I knew through me their game could be lifted higher, and through that sense of team we would be successful.

I realized I'd not just relied on Tauj; I'd made her my crutch. I'd leaned on her for a long time in every way, and in doing so I was limiting what God had for me. I think God dares us to step out on our own in life. He's saying, "Trust me, I've got you." As you do so, yes, there can be doubt (sure was for me), but you find out God has given you what you need to succeed. I was a stronger person than I knew. Not just in basketball but also in *life*.

In Texas, I found something I didn't expect. I found my-self. I had to ask and answer all kinds of questions: *Who am I going to be? What am I going to stand for? Where am I going to go? What am I going to do with what I have and who I am?* I hadn't chosen detachment from Tauj, just like she hadn't chosen to abandon me. We each chose a different path that would allow us to live out our very best.

And in that, God was helping me find my own self, my own talent, and my own potential.

In my senior year at Duncanville, everyone was determined to do something about the disappointing ending of the year before.

Coach Hackerott put in new offensive plays designed to optimize the talents of our best players. In addition to our standard offensive plays, where we would pass and dribble the ball around to find the open player, there were now new offense sets that stacked the play in favor of a particular player. Coach would say it was designed to allow any particular player to create her own offense, to make her own play, and to score on the basis of her own talent.

Coach would say later that that was a lot to ask of juniors and seniors in high school—to manage two different offenses and to switch them on the fly—but we were up to the task. And while it was difficult for us to execute, it was even harder to defend against.

I don't think I was aware that Coach Hackerott was putting in these plays for me at the time. Others on our team were good as well, and the plays could be run through them also. But I later learned that Coach really designed these offensive sets for my sake, to optimize my talents on the court. And to some degree, she had to do so, because before I hadn't been taking the shots during games I could have and should have.

We started the season by winning. And winning some more.

It wasn't just the new offense that got us wins. In fact, we used it selectively. We had a strong team, and we were good.

One oddity of that year was a game where I was able to score a "quintuple-double." People refer to a double-double as a game where a player scores in double digits in two statistical categories—for example, ten or more points and ten or more steals. Sometimes you hear of a triple-double. For that there are five overall statistical categories: points, rebounds, assists, steals, and blocks. And in one game in 1997, I scored double digits in all five categories. What can I say? I was everywhere, and the passion that I play with was seen in every play—offensively and defensively.

Duncanville plowed through the regular season, living up to the high reputation of Duncanville girls' basketball from years before. And by the end of the regular season, we were undefeated. How far would we go this year?

We were determined not to get sabotaged by an early ejection from the playoffs. And we didn't. In fact, we breezed through the playoffs, beating opponents by a dozen or so points each time. And we landed in the finals, facing a very strong team from Alief Elsik.

The championship game in Austin, Texas, was hard-fought. Alief Elsik was a very good team. They were as strong a defensive team as we'd played all year. And we might have been dealing with nerves and the game hype at the outset.

We kept the game close, but it wasn't until halfway through the second quarter that we started playing *our* game, not just playing *a* game.

We would lead the game much of the rest of the way, but we never led by a lot. And we all knew that in the final minutes of any basketball game a team can lose through bad foul shooting or getting rattled by a full-court press.

At one point in the final minutes, during a time-out, Coach Hackerott pulled me aside. "When the ball comes to you," she said, "take it to the basket. They can't stop you."

This wasn't our standard offense and it wasn't the new offense. Coach was making it the "Tamika" offense. For the shy team player I was, this was difficult. I wanted so much to play the team game. And this was in the highest-pressure moment of the whole season, and of my entire high school basketball career.

Coach was giving me permission to take over the game. She was putting the ball into my hands and telling me to win the game.

Back on the court, we advanced the ball, and soon enough the ball came to me. I held it a minute on the perimeter, my defender playing me tough. But I saw my advantage, nudged left but dribbled right, and quickly sliced past into the lane, dribbling around another player. I launched myself toward the basket in one, two leaping steps, finally able to bank the ball and see it fall through the net.

I can't say that was the turning point in the game, though perhaps it was the point when we really took control. But it was a turning point for me. It was a moment when I could bear the weight of a team on my own shoulders and perform at my greatest ability to score and lead us to a win.

Both the concept of team and the concept of leadership are important. In many ways, my future career in basketball would become a pendulum swing between both, and I would learn lesson after lesson about each one as I grew in my abilities and opportunities.

Yes, we won the championship game.

For me, it was some measure of accomplishment to win state, fulfilling my dad's wishes, although a year late. I also found some satisfaction in winning two state titles in different states, Illinois and Texas.

Winning this way—after leaving my team of the Catchings Sisters behind, discovering a new team in Duncanville, and then stepping up in my senior year to be a leader, as shy and young and uncomfortable as I was—felt good.

And now as I looked forward to graduating from high school, the question was not what I would do with my life. The only question was where I would play.

7

CHOSEN

Picture a kid with a smile as pure and unaffected
as early morning sun, and that was Tamika . . .
Picture too, a young woman who hid behind her
openness. Who, despite the sociable veneer, would
often sit withdrawn and alone on her high school
bus, writing in a notebook.

    Pat Summitt, head coach, Tennessee Lady Vols

I vividly remember watching TV one evening back in eighth
grade. I was flipping the channels—and then stopped, becoming suddenly mesmerized by one person. I thought, *Oh,
wow. Who is this?*

    Blue eyes filled the whole screen. Steely blue eyes—not cold,
not icy blue, but the blue you see in a fire. So intense you could
feel the heat six hundred miles away, through the screen, the
crowd, and the cameras. Those eyes arrested me, stopped me

from changing the channel, and as the camera pulled back and showed the whole face, I sat up and leaned toward the TV.

Everybody always talks about Pat Summitt's glare, but nothing prepares you for it. Seeing it for the first time, on TV, and not even directed at me, I thought, *Man, I never want that kind of stare-down, because the way she can look at you will leave a hole.* In a way, as I sat there on the couch, her stare already had gone through me. She wasn't giving me the eye, but those eyes on that screen? I could feel them. I was completely mesmerized and even a little afraid.

And drawn in.

She speaks my language, I thought. Pat could say volumes without speaking a single word like no one else I'd ever seen. She didn't have to voice her thoughts. Those eyes, that jaw, the set of her mouth, the hallmark stance, standing so tall, arms folded across her torso as if to hold in this extraordinary energy that would surely erupt otherwise—man, that said everything. She was zeroed-in, concerned, absolutely extraordinary.

I was completely smitten with that kind of passion. I recognized it. It was inside me too. I wanted more of it. Seeing that kind of intensity from a woman coach in action, I was blown away.

I dropped the remote control and stayed fixed on the rest of the game. The camera pulled back and panned a crowd going crazy over some call. The players huddled, then slipped back to their places on the court as the screen zoomed out even more and went completely orange. Playing on their home court, the Lady Volunteers of the University of Tennessee were swathed in orange: orange sweatshirts, T-shirts, hats, hair, jackets, face paint, posters, pompoms, banners.

The school doesn't use the tagline "Big Orange. Big Ideas" for nothing. Fans bear the color proudly. It was impressive and bright and seared itself into my dreams.

Pat stalked the sidelines like a lion. I began to watch her almost more than the game itself. She's not this giant woman, just five foot eleven, I would learn later. But she has this huge presence. Big. Inescapable. She could do that stare-down one moment, then stand graceful and serene the next. Minutes later she was hugging a player tight, warmly, so . . . motherly. I'd never seen anyone coach like she did. She breathed life into that game, those players. There was a respect from her and toward her from everyone in the crowd, even the opposing team. She was a tidal wave, altogether so very human and a force of nature.

That was my introduction, at the age of thirteen, to the legendary Pat Summitt, head coach of the University of Tennessee Lady Volunteers and women's basketball icon.

Coach Summitt's piercing eyes swept across the court, and the TV camera happened to catch her steely gaze. For a half second, it was as if she was looking through the camera, into our TV, and right at me.

Yes, ma'am, I thought to myself. *I want to play for you.*

Three years later, at the end of my junior year at Duncanville, my future was more complicated.

I was very much on the radar of college recruiters. After my sophomore year at Stevenson with Tauja, the national championship, the Ms. Illinois Basketball award, and the opportunities growing every day my junior year at Duncanville, I was being watched by college coaches all over the country.

There were rules governing how college coaches could approach prospective players. They couldn't make personal, in-person contact until the player's senior year. But in one's junior year, schools could issue letters of interest.

And as a junior, I found letters of interest started piling into our mailbox. Mom set up blue plastic Rubbermaid containers to hold them all.

Every day, schools I'd never even thought about offered scholarships to play for their teams. I was amazed . . . and proud. All my work I believed would add up to something finally had. If my game on the court hadn't been enough to convince others of my worth, the stack of recruitment letters spoke volumes.

Mom and I would sit at the table to open and read the letters together till it became overwhelming. How to respond?

"The first thing you do is be grateful," Mom said. "Thank everyone who extends you such generosity."

I was grateful and humbled to be thought of, invited, and welcomed to every one of those schools. I began to write my thanks by hand. All the while, I wondered, *What do I want?*

Tauj and I hadn't forgotten the pact we'd made to play together again in college. It wasn't about a reunion of the "Catchings Sisters." It was about family. Getting the family together again. Tauj and me.

A year ahead of me, she was close to making her choice. Though we'd made that pact, we'd hadn't talked specifically about what school she was thinking about. The talks we did have were more about my own struggle to choose. The decision seemed so weighty for me. Ultimately, I had my eyes on the fact that where I went to college could enhance or hinder my chances of becoming an NBA pro someday.

The year after I left Stevenson, Tauja led the school to its second straight championship and won the Ms. Illinois Basketball award. We kept it in the family. I didn't know for sure where she might go to college, but Illinois had become her home. Meanwhile, Tauj knew I leaned toward Tennessee. I'd made that known since eighth grade—I often talked about Pat Summitt and the Tennessee Lady Vols. Kenyon even gave me a University of Tennessee sweatshirt one Christmas. I wore it everywhere.

But was it more important for Tauj and me to play somewhere together? And wouldn't it be so fun to be in college together?

Tauja was close to deciding.

Something inside me told me I should work at making my decision too. So I thought hard about all the options. I leaned heavily toward the University of Tennessee from the start, but I also held onto letters from the University of Southern California and the University of Arkansas.

And then I learned Tauja had made her choice: the University of Illinois.

I was shocked. She signed without even a conversation with me. *What about our pact?*

I felt pressured to look at the University of Illinois. I flipped through the stack of recruiting offers in the blue bin. I knew there was one there from the University of Illinois. I pulled it from the stack and read it again.

Looks like I'll be visiting Champaign too, I said to myself. I took the letter to my room and added it to the three others. But I never told Tauj.

The day I made my recruitment visit, Tauja had no idea I was in Illinois. Another player was there as well, and we were given a tour of the school and then invited to meet the team. The players walked into the room and the coach started introducing us.

Tauja squealed my name and ran to me. "What are you doing here?" she asked, hugging me tight.

I laughed. "I'm one of the recruits."

"I knew we were going to meet some recruits this weekend," she said, "but no one told me one would be you." She gave me a look with raised eyebrows.

So much had happened so quickly. Tauja had started college and I was ending high school, and we both were just trying to keep up with the schoolwork, our sports, the new demands and plans and expectations. The split two years before and the distance by four states had put some challenges between us, but never a wall. It felt so good to be side by side again, talking basketball and school.

But I also thought how different we were now than in our high school days as the Catchings Sisters. I was stronger and more confident, and Tauj was different too. But our bond would never be broken. I felt the same closeness as ever to Tauj. We'd just each moved toward our separate goals in life, and we wanted different things. I realized we'd chosen them with that first split.

So we chatted with everyone and laughed and talked about basketball, and it was a good time. But I knew right away the University of Illinois wasn't the place I wanted to be. A piece of my heart was with Tennessee the first day I saw Pat Summitt's intensity and the Lady Vols orange light up the television screen. And since my moment back in eighth grade, Coach Summitt had only become more legendary.

Toward the end of our day, away from everyone, Tauj and I got a chance to talk. I studied her face. She knew. She always does. She made it easy.

She looked me straight in the eye. "Don't come here for me. You know if you come here, you'll have to play another year after I'm gone. Come here only if you want to be here." She paused a moment and smiled. "If this isn't the place you want to be, I'm okay with you going where you want to go."

I nodded.

"'Cause I know," she said, "that's the University of Tennessee."

Shortly after our volleyball championship win my junior year, Coach Pat Summitt and her assistant coach and recruiter, Mickie DeMoss, came for what was called an in-home visit. We planned to meet at the local mall before heading home to complete the rest of the visit.

I walked through the mall pinching myself and trying to figure out if this was real. The woman who had mesmerized me on TV years ago was now in Duncanville to see . . . *me?* Dreams really do come true. I think all the anxiety and waiting is what made me start to feel sick. Out of nowhere I got a migraine headache, and I felt my brain shutting down. Then I saw her. In my head I was chanting, *Oh my, oh my, oh my,* but I managed to squeak out a "Hi, Coach" as we approached each other. This had to be the best moment in my life and a step closer to my dreams and goals.

When we arrived back at the house, while Mom and Pat sat in the dining room talking, I invited Coach DeMoss to my bedroom to show her some of my stuff. My wall was covered with items and photos of people that inspired me—inspirational quotes along with my purple and turquoise Charlotte Hornets paraphernalia were all over the place. There was also my USA Junior National team jersey and right there in the corner was my first letter from the University of Tennessee, signed by Mickie DeMoss. We talked for a long time.

The thing I remember most about Pat on her visit to my house was her sincerity and honesty. She sat me down and looked into my eyes with an intense but easy stare.

She said, "Tamika, now, you could want me to promise you playing time and promise you a starting position, but the reality is—I can't. Just like every other player who has played for me, you will have to earn your minutes and your position. You will have to fight every day to be the best you can be. But one thing I can promise you is that I will help make you the best player you can be."

I don't think I had any doubt I wanted to go to Tennessee, but I didn't know for sure that they would want me. Only later would we learn they wanted me badly but they were resigned to the idea that I would likely go to Illinois to be reunited with Tauja.

Mickie DeMoss tells how she and Coach Summitt took a side trip to Chicago to talk with my dad. They didn't want to get to the end of the process of winning me over and then face a dad who was opposed to the choice. Mickie and Pat walked away feeling that Dad wouldn't oppose Tennessee if it were truly my choice.

And it was my choice: Tennessee. I know Dad might have preferred me going to Illinois, but he didn't get in the way of my decision.

What did get in the way was a snafu at Tennessee regarding my acceptance letter. I waited and waited for a confirmation that they were admitting me. They had my letter declaring they were my choice. But nothing came in reply.

Turns out there was a clerical error, and my letter had been overlooked. Once that was sorted out, I heard back from them. From Coach Summitt herself.

I read and reread her letter. Could this be real? I looked again at the letterhead, black with orange; the signature, bold and slanted slightly left; the large loop for the *P* and at the bottom of the *S*; the full name, formal and clear with her official title printed underneath. I shook my head. Her full title . . . as if I wouldn't know who she was.

This was what I had dreamed about three years earlier when I first saw Pat Summitt on TV. I reread that letter one more time, looked again at her signature, and pinned it next to my seventh-grade goal, which I'd moved to a special corner wall of my bedroom.

8

TENNESSEE

> The result of all this need and emotion was a team
> of swift, rippling electricity. The "Three Meeks,"
> Semeka, Tamika, and Chamique, floated across
> the floor creating one unbelievable play after an-
> other; the ball would go flying up the court from
> Meek to Meek and never hit the ground. It was
> like watching volleyball.
>
> Pat Summitt, *Sum It Up*

For me, the road to college basketball was . . . Interstate 40.

Mom and I drove from Duncanville to the University of
Tennessee in Knoxville, and it took us just shy of thirteen
hours. I don't know if the drive seemed longer to her or to
me. I was on the brink of realizing a huge dream: Tennessee.
Mom was losing her daughter.

I was maybe a little nervous stepping into this new location, new level, and new life, but I had no regrets. There was

no looking back. This is what I had hoped for and planned for. I could hardly wait to get there.

The year before, the Tennessee Lady Vols, under Coach Pat Summitt, went 29–10 and ran the table in the NCAA Tournament, defeating Old Dominion in the championship game. It was Coach Summitt's fifth national championship and the second year in a row that she'd won it. Women's basketball at Tennessee was the best in the country. Pat Summitt had already become a legend in the college ranks, and she was gaining national recognition even from those who didn't follow women's collegiate basketball.

This was the program I was stepping into. As Mom and I watched the dry dust of Texas through the rearview mirror and the green hills of Arkansas whiz past our car windows, I knew I was riding into a great opportunity, the dream of a lifetime. And also a challenging future.

But it was the dream *I had pursued*. I wanted this. I wanted to shoot for the best. I wanted to play for the best coach, with the best players, and against the best players.

Tennessee represented all of that to me.

I think sometimes we settle for less than we should. We're scared of challenges, afraid we might fail. Sometimes we settle in at a level where we're confident we'll compete well—maybe at a level beneath the talents God has given us. But it's comfortable for us, and we know at that level we might just avoid the pain of failure.

But then how will we know what we could have been?

Mom turned off Interstate 40 onto Henley Street, which led directly into the campus of the University of Tennessee. She had tears in her eyes. I had stars in mine.

So I'd be playing with the best, against the best. What would that make me?

Better.

I had been to the campus before, but now it seemed all the more beautiful and impressive—dotted with green lawns, lined with trees, and bounded by the Tennessee River to the east. A number of the buildings were older, with a kind of southern gothic look to them, but the dorm I'd be living in—Humes Hall—was modern, with a tall glass-and-steel face and clean, contemporary design inside.

I don't remember the exact sequence of events that first day on campus, except for locating the dorm, finding my room, and Mom and me unpacking the car.

I remember connecting with my roommates—who would also be my teammates—some of whom I'd known from USA Basketball and the Nike High School All-American team we'd played on.

I remember feeling a little overwhelmed. I was prepared to work really hard, but I didn't know what I was walking into. This was the big time. The campus was big. The buildings were big. The basketball arena was big. I would be living in one of a bazillion dorms.

I remember also feeling content, in a way, that after a long process of dreaming about this, it was actually happening. I was finally here.

The next day Mom helped me get settled in my dorm room. We did some shopping and we talked. She would later say that, for her, it was like "mission accomplished." She had endured a lot, gone through the ups and downs of life with me. We had survived, in a way, the split of the family. Now she would be alone.

I remember her saying good-bye to me. Kisses. Tears. I walked back to the dorm, realizing I'd come a long way from being a short, skinny girl with big box hearing aids. I had overcome much, accomplished a lot, and now would achieve more. I was on my own.

I remember turning my head one last time. Mom was gone.

One of my teammates, Chamique Holdsclaw, was the veteran of the team. She was a junior and had led the Lady Vols to two previous championships. She was what I would call an "outgoing introvert." A lot like me. She was reserved, cherishing times by herself, but was also a leader by example. Over the two years we played together at Tennessee, I would learn a lot from her.

Chamique was the best player in college basketball. Period. She had been called the "Michael Jordan of college basketball." She was that good. Most of us coming in thought playing with her—or against her—was the Holy Grail of our young basketball careers.

Semeka Randall was, like me, a freshman recruit. She was an All-American, and had played ball in high school in Ohio. I'd played with her the previous two summers on the Junior National teams (now called U18 and U19), so we already knew each other. A defensive stopper, she would become known as "The Glove." Semeka was the most outgoing of our group, always the center of attention, the one most likely to "get the party started" in many ways, and on the court as well.

Because of our names—Chamique, Semeka, and Tamika—the three of us quickly became labeled in the media as "the Meeks." Former star player and then basketball commentator Nancy Lieberman would, on ESPN, call us "the Meeka Club." Since Chamique was a junior and would graduate sooner, we "Meeks" would be together for only two years, but in that short time we'd make our identity known.

The freshman class Coach Summitt had recruited that year consisted of me and Semeka, Teresa Geter, a towering center, and Kristen "Ace" Clement, a point guard from Philly.

Pat Summitt had had her eye on all four of us for years. This particular year, four of Coach Summitt's prime recruits had all said yes to Tennessee. It was an unprecedented recruiting class, exceeding even Coach's own dreams. Some in the media were already calling us the "best recruiting class in college basketball ever."

Teresa Geter had ruled South Carolina basketball the previous four years. She was a center-forward and stood taller than the rest of us at about six four. We called her "Tree." Kristen Clement had been a standout in Philadelphia, breaking Wilt Chamberlain's high school scoring record. Something like 2,200 points. Crazy-good numbers. Her brother had given her the nickname "Ace" and it stuck.

Ace and I would be roommates and begin a friendship that lasts to this day.

So the four of us freshmen—me, Semeka, Tree, and Ace—settled into our rooms at Humes Hall, where we'd live together for the next year, a year that would bond us in ways that we would not yet imagine could be possible.

But we weren't thinking about that. We were already itching to play some hoops.

I don't remember if it was our first night there, but it was pretty close to it. We freshmen, dubbed the Fab 4 by the media, found ourselves at the HPER Athletic Center on the court with our upperclassmen teammates. This included Chamique Holdsclaw, Kellie Jolly, Kyra Elzy, and a few others.

It was meant to be a friendly, casual shoot-around. At least it started that way.

Someone suggested we play a pickup game against each other. And then someone else suggested it be the upperclassmen against the freshmen. And suddenly there was an edge to the competition. There was a lot to prove.

Apparently, there had also been talk swirling about Chamique and me. Some people had suggested there would inevitably be competition, jealousy, and turf wars, and that the team couldn't hold us both.

This wasn't the first time I'd met Chamique. In my junior year of high school, I'd visited the campus of the University of Tennessee. It was part of any college-bound kid's normal process. It was also an opportunity for the school to recruit possible players. Chamique was active in that recruiting process, writing letters and telling potential recruits about her experience of the school and what it was like playing there. At one point, Chamique and I had time to talk about more personal issues, including our family situations. We had things in common besides basketball.

So I never understood why people thought Chamique and I would be at odds. People who said that never really knew me. And they probably didn't know Chamique. Jealousy and turf wars, no way.

Competition, yes. Of course. Not for bragging rights,

but just because we relished the challenge of playing against the best.

And so we played that night. The upperclassmen were going to show the freshmen what college basketball was all about. But we freshmen were bound and determined to show them why we were there.

We played man-to-man. I was assigned to play Chamique. At first, we freshmen were overwhelmed. After all, these upperclassmen had played together for a couple of years. We were playing against the best.

Although we started slowly, we soon picked up the pace. We became more competitive. Semeka taunted the others about letting the freshmen show them up. More trash talk and hard play followed.

Chamique and I played hard against each other and enjoyed it. Chamique was obviously a great player, but I did well enough against her. I'd fly around her for a layup, but then she'd pull up and nail a pinpoint three.

We played for maybe an hour—hard, tough basketball, friendly but fierce, a game to demonstrate ourselves to each other. In the end, we knew our upperclassmen teammates were awfully good. The upperclassmen, on the other hand, got their heads turned by us freshmen and learned firsthand why all four of us had been high school all-stars.

As for the game itself, I don't remember who won. But I think in the end it was Tennessee.

In 1997, Coach Pat Summitt was a living legend in women's basketball[1] and on her way to staking a respected place among the elite coaches of both the women's and the men's games.

She had played for University of Tennessee-Martin in the early seventies,[2] and set records there that still stand. In 1974, the same year she graduated, she was named coach of the Tennessee Lady Vols at a grand salary of $250 a month.[3] In those first years of coaching, her players were only a year or two younger than she was.

She built the Tennessee women's basketball program from scratch (at one point funding new uniforms by means of a doughnut sale), and by the time I got there more than two decades later, she had amassed six SEC titles, two SEC Coach of the Year awards, and had led the U.S. team to gold in the 1984 Los Angeles Olympics. From 1977 to 1980 she compiled a 30–2 record as coach of United States teams involved in international competition.

And, oh yes, her Tennessee Lady Vols had already won the NCCA Championship five times. And that included championships each of the two years before I came.

No pressure.

At five eleven, Summitt stood an inch or so under many of her players, including me, but when she spoke, most of us felt like she was seven feet tall. I easily recalled my experience of watching her on TV when I was young, and I quickly realized she was exactly that same person. She really did have blue eyes the color of lasers; they could bore holes through steel—and through freshmen basketball players. It was Niya Butts, freshman forward on the 1996–1997 championship team, who, after a halftime lecture from Summitt, would comment, "I don't think she blinks when she talks."[4]

Pat Summitt's sheer will to win seemed always coiled up in her athletic body, and it would unleash at a moment's notice. She would put up with cold shooting and the occasional messed-up pass on the offensive end. But if you didn't get back down the court to play good defense, that's when she'd call a time-out and the yelling would begin. Her eyes would grow to the size of Frisbees and those laser blues of hers would begin drilling holes in you.

One of Pat Summitt's mottos was "To be the best you have to play the best." It led her from the beginning to build up Tennessee's level of competition, including creating the rivalry with UConn that began in 1995.

Yes, she was Pat Summitt.

Leader.

Lady Vol.

Legend.

And during my first practice at the University of Tennessee, she was the force of nature I would dare to defy.

In high school, I'd never really been told I was doing anything wrong in my basketball technique. I was successful, and I suppose the coaches thought what I was doing was working. They probably thought, *If she ain't broke, don't fix her*. And my game was pretty good—successful enough to get me the phone call from Pat Summitt and a ticket to play for the best program in college basketball.

When I got to Tennessee, I kind of thought I had it down, this basketball thing. I was there because I was already good and accomplished in the sport.

And so, when I walked into basketball practice in Tennessee's Thompson-Boling Arena for the first time, I guess I was expecting the playing technique I'd brought with me would be perfectly fine.

One of the things I wasn't used to was open practice. Especially for the first practice of the year, Coach would open it up to spectators. So when we walked onto the court to run drills, there was an audience—season ticket holders, alumnae, students, faculty, media. And because of the success of the Lady Vols in previous years, there was public interest in this new 1997 version of the team. A hundred or so onlookers watched our practice.

We lined up for one of the defensive drills. Two lines facing each other on the right side of the basket, one offense and one defense. One from each line would peel off against each other, one-on-one, the offensive player cutting toward the basket in a zigzag, with the player from the other line defending.

So when I was up, I defended in my usual way—straight up, super-aggressive, going after the ball. The offensive player zigzagged and I kept pace.

I heard a whistle blow. "Stop!"

We stopped the drill and looked over. It was Pat, her laser eyes bearing down on me.

"Bend your knees," she said to me. "Arms out. Move with the player."

She came over and positioned me, pushing me down so my knees were bent and lifting my arms so they were straight out. "Slide," she said, "with the player."

I don't remember if I said anything. I wasn't used to being singled out and corrected. With a big gulp I whispered "Okay." I got through and went to the back of the line.

When I was back at the front of the line, I positioned myself on defense. We did it again. Pat blew her whistle again.

"Stop!"

And again, Pat was looking straight at me. "I just told you," she said with a little more impatient edge in her voice. "Bend your knees. Arms out. Move with the player. Use your wing span." Blinking back tears, I got through it and went to the back of the line.

I was getting frustrated. What I was doing was giving me a good chance of stealing the ball. I was being aggressive on defense, doing what I knew to be successful for years in high school. Pat was forcing me to do it another way I thought was not going to be nearly as successful.

As I got back up to the front of the line, I looked up. Pat was at the area behind the basket, talking with a few people.

I was bound and determined to get through this drill so we could hopefully move on to the next one—especially since she wasn't looking. And so once again I did it my way.

But I swear Pat had eyes in the back of her head. Just as I was in my defensive stance, the Tamika Catchings stance, she turned to watch.

I did it again. And again Pat blew her whistle.

"Stop!"

Now she was really steamed. "Catch!" she yelled. "How many times do I have to tell you?"

And this time I yelled back, "But it doesn't work *that* way!"

And suddenly there was silence. The spectators, the team, everyone just stopped. Everyone was looking for the battle starting to unfold. You could literally hear a pin drop.

It was one of those moments. Just one moment, but it felt like five minutes. No one dared to talk back to Coach Summitt. While I faced the stare-down, in my mind I was kicking and screaming at myself. I couldn't believe I lost my cool—on the first day of practice.

Finally, Pat motioned for the drill to start back up, but called me underneath the basket to talk to her.

In her cool demeanor, with her eyes piercing through my body, she asked low so only I could hear, "Do I need to send you back to Duncanville, Texas?" It came across as less of a question, and more like a threat.

I'm thinking, *I can't believe I talked back to her like that.* "No, ma'am," I replied. *If I get sent back home, Mom's gonna kill me!*

Coach continued: "Am I gonna have to handle you with lace gloves?" She drew out the words "lace gloves" in a derisive tone. She had a thing against the word *girl*—the use of the word to mean a female who couldn't compete as men did, tough and competitive and fierce. "Lace gloves" was her way of saying, "Are you going to play like a girl?"

I was furious and frustrated. "I'm not used to being yelled at like that!"

"Am I not supposed to coach you?" Coach Summitt said. "Am I not supposed to do my job? Am I going to have this problem with you all year?"

"No, ma'am."

"I'll send you right back to Texas. You need to stop being stubborn and start thinking about this team. You're going to get yourself in trouble. You're going to get the team in trouble." Pat then added coolly, "We don't need to have this conversation again." She turned without saying another word to me.

After practice, I showered and dressed, then went up to Coach Summitt's office.

I apologized. "I'm sorry, Coach," I said. "I got frustrated. It will never happen again."

And it didn't. That would be my first—and last—run-in with Coach Summitt in my entire college career.

Like I said, I wasn't used to being told I was doing something wrong. But it went deeper than that. I wasn't used to being yelled at. That hurt me. And in that first practice, I had suddenly felt that my coach was singling me out and yelling at me, humiliating me in front of others.

I realized later that wasn't her intent. I realized I had defied her authority and she couldn't allow that, for the sake of the team.

I also didn't realize at that point how much Coach Summitt specialized in defense. She believed offense would usually take care of itself. There were offensive strategies, of course—plays designed to get the best-shooting players into their best position to take their best shot. And in that moment, offense was one-on-one—a great player jumping and shooting over a defender.

Defense, Coach knew, needed to be a team effort. A hotshot player like me trying to play one-on-one defense might succeed once in a while in stealing the ball, but all those other times she would lunge at the ball unsuccessfully, setting up the rest of the team to defend four against five.

My initial defiance of Coach Summitt was an opportunity for her to make a statement. Tennessee was going to play defense and it was going to play it the right way. Pat Summitt's way. She used my defiance to make a statement. She knew I would back down.

Pat had counted on that.

For me, it was a lesson learned. Or maybe I should say, a lesson I would continue to learn. And it's a life lesson too.

Life isn't played solo. We need people around us, family, and friends.

Teammates in life.

I've been asked who my best friend was in college. Not dodging the question, but the truth is I had a number of "best friends."

Now, of course, all of us on the team were friends in a special way. When you practice with others so often in the course of a week, your teammates become your social life, your "sorority," your world. So we were all close in the way teammates are.

But the four of us freshmen became especially good friends, in part because we were living together in Humes Hall. The dorm layout was a suite of rooms: a center hallway with a sink on one end and a shower on the other, and two doors each suited with double beds. Semeka and Tree shared one of the rooms. Ace and I shared the other.

While Pat Summitt was famous for not liking or using the word *girl*, we Fab 4 freshmen got to hang out together just as girls. We practiced together, ate together, and talked together—about school, family, guys, and boyfriends.

My roommate Kristen probably resented the girly-girl image as much as Coach did. She was naturally beautiful and had won some beauty contests in high school. But that beauty queen stereotype seemed to overshadow her athleticism and hard work on the basketball court. She was good—really good—as a scoring leader and record breaker in Philadelphia high school basketball, and she wanted to be known for the athleticism she had worked for and earned, not for the beauty she was born with.

Ace, Semeka, and I had played together before Tennessee—at the Junior Nationals that previous summer. That was a whirlwind eight days, and it didn't give us a chance to develop close friendships, but it was a confidence builder as we competed against some of the best in the world and walked away with a championship.

Falling short of making the Junior Nationals team, Tree hadn't had that experience. And in that first year at Tennessee, she struggled to find herself. As we all settled into dorm life, Tree always seemed a little aloof. I think she wasn't sure she was good enough to deserve being there.

One night Semeka came to Ace and me and told us Tree was crying. She had studied hard for a biology exam, but it was a tough subject for her, and she was terrified of failing. What's more, tomorrow was her birthday, but she thought no one knew.

Semeka said, "We have to do something."

The next afternoon, Semeka, Ace, and I planned a surprise. That night we were all together with Tree, acting like it was just another night in the dorm. We talked about eating out—but no, by design Semeka, Ace, and I voted that down. Instead we decided to order pizza. And all along Tree was thinking, *It's my birthday and no one cares.*

When the pizza was delivered, we called Tree into Ace's and my room. There in the dark was a birthday cake aflame with candles. Tree's eyes filled with tears and she was overwhelmed by what we'd done. Semeka started to sing, but not "Happy Birthday." It was the song "Count on Me" from the movie *Waiting to Exhale*.

We all joined in, singing as best we could through tears, "The friendship that will never end."

Semeka, on the other hand, quickly gained notice on the court for being fast and relentless. Her speed was an injection of energy whenever she was brought into a game—the opposing players literally could not keep up with her. In high school, and now in college, Semeka would turn out to be one of the game's fiercest defenders, setting records for steals and proving to bring far more than opposing players could handle.

Of course, to us in Humes Hall, Semeka was just one of us girls. She was one of the Fab 4. One of the four freshmen with a chance to make history.

Coach expected a lot out of us. That goes without saying when you're talking about a legend. But in practices she drove us to our limits and beyond.

I knew two things: I had never had to work that hard. And I loved the challenge.

Early on, Coach made a simple comment: "I hope you're in shape." She dropped it out there in front of us like it was a spare dime that had fallen out of her purse. Of course, it wasn't casual or carelessly spoken. It was completely intentional on her part. Only, we freshmen didn't know that.

What we did know was from Kyra Elzy, a returning sophomore, who had played with us at the Junior Nationals in the summer. She had talked about the grueling nature of Pat Summitt's practices—the endless wind sprints and six a.m. runs around the track. We were told conditioning was the name of her game and that she was relentless about it.

What we heard scared us. We had visions of Coach Summitt practices that were so exhausting we'd wind up puking in the corners of the gym. And so, to avoid that humiliation, the four of us freshmen started conditioning ourselves before we got to practice.

What we didn't know was that there was a tradition among upperclassmen on the team to do their best to terrify the freshmen. And I'm not so sure Pat didn't put Kyra up to that.

It worked. We freshmen were doing our own conditioning before conditioning started.

I'm sure Pat had counted on that. She wanted your all. Everything about her said, "I want to make you better." Everything we did had a purpose—to make us all better.

I remember how tough it was, but it was tough in a good way. I loved it. I don't think you go to a top school like the University of Tennessee and a top program with a top coach without knowing four demands:

1. You're gonna have to work really, really hard.
2. You're gonna have to make certain sacrifices.
3. You're gonna have a learning curve, jumping you up to a new level.
4. You're gonna have to work really, really hard.

And so, having gotten ourselves conditioned to endure a Pat Summitt practice, we practiced hard. Coach sometimes had us practicing against a squad consisting of all men, knowing that their height and strength on the court would condition us well.

One-on-one with each other, there was no telling what might happen. It was very competitive between us. After all, for many of us, especially us freshmen, we were excited to be there, but not so sure we were going to fit. And how would we be able to shine with so much talent on the court? So we fought and battled and competed hard. There was blood shed every day in practice. And it was emotional too. Lots of competition, wanting to prove ourselves against someone else.

Sometimes that emotional competition would get carried off the court. Women tend to hold on to stuff. But Coach Summitt wouldn't allow that. She tried to make sure nothing interpersonal festered and stewed between us.

When we got off the court, we were family.

And at the end of the days of practice, we had worked so hard, built up our stamina so high, fought so intensely, that when we got to games, in terms of conditioning, they were relatively easy.

And, again, I'm pretty sure Pat had counted on that.

Part 3

MUSIC

The rhythm . . . the flow . . . the beat . . .
Every note becomes a bar
Every bar forms into a song
As the orchestra flows, I see the ball move . . .
Effortless
One pass. Two pass. Three pass goes . . .
Swish, swish, swish it's like a melody that flows.

Getting ready to attack
Sitting back and being blessed
God's choices of who gets what
Displayed throughout the game.
This is the skill that's been select
All I do is focus on what's next
Shoot, drive, pass, slide . . .
Decisions to be made
At a drop of a dime.
Hearts racing
Hands flailing
Drops falling from my face.
Shirts soaking
Shoes squeaking
Love's captured in my veins.
I'm ready . . .

9

PERFECT

Four freshmen and a sophomore, Kyra Elzy, were leading our comeback over the best team in the country. No sooner had the thought occurred to me than Tamika Catchings paused from three-point range. She squared up. Then she floated upwards and launched a long bomb. It fluttered through the net, and the arena erupted.

Pat Summitt, *Raise the Roof*

The Thompson-Boling Arena was built in 1987 specifically for basketball. Designed as an octagon, it rises impressively right along the Tennessee River. Seating some twenty-five thousand people, it's the biggest arena in Tennessee and one of the largest in the South.

It was a twelve-minute walk from our dorm.

I remember my first time entering the place. I had played in a lot of arenas and wasn't usually affected much by the size of a venue. A basketball court is always the same size, wherever you play. But Thompson-Boling was really something. I don't think I was overwhelmed by it or that I had doubts about my being there, but it made me catch my breath. Made me think about where I'd come from. What, with God's help, I had been able to achieve so far.

Early polls had us ranked number one or number two, alongside frequent Tennessee nemesis Louisiana Tech. When the season opened, *Sports Illustrated* had picked Tech to win the national championship, but everyone knew we were a close number two.

After weeks of practice, we were ready to play. Or so we thought. In a way, every team is just a collection of statistics before its first game. We had some of the best talent in the country, stars from every region of the United States, now living and practicing together in Knoxville, Tennessee. On paper, we were terrific. We had so much talent. But, of course, four of us had yet to play a single minute in college. You never know how it will come together. *If* it will come together. What we were on paper didn't count. As someone once said, "That's why you have to play the games."

We'd had an early exhibition game against the U.S. Armed Forces team. It wasn't much of a competition—we won 111–54. I'm sure Pat was glad she could get all of us playing time and that we got through it without any injuries.

Well, sort of.

Early in November, Kristen Clement hurt her foot. At first it was just a sore foot, but later, while running wind sprints,

Ace felt some pain. Later an MRI revealed it was a stress fracture. While it wasn't so serious as to keep her out for a long time, she would certainly miss the first game against Mississippi. What was more concerning was our second game—an early head-to-head against our top competition—Louisiana Tech. And that was only three days after the Mississippi game. Was there any chance Ace would be back by then?

We would have to start our season without our new point guard. The much-hyped "reveal" of the Fab 4 freshman class—Semeka, Tree, Ace, and me—would not happen. Not yet.

Coach Summitt started four of her veterans and me in the game against Ole Miss. Kellie Jolly, a junior, started at point guard.

We started slowly. I don't know why—first-game nerves, still-developing chemistry?—but after four minutes, the score was 4–2. It wasn't supposed to start this way.

Pat put Semeka Randall in the game. Semeka's game is one of intense energy and enthusiasm, which we really needed. In a short time, defensive phenom Semeka, "the Glove," grabbed two steals and drove repeatedly for layups. Six minutes later, we had gone on a 15–0 run, with Ole Miss scoring zero points.

In the end, that first game wasn't even close. We won 92–54. In retrospect, it wasn't a game that proved much; Mississippi finished last in the SEC that year and wasn't strong competition for us. But we still needed to play the games, and as our first game, it proved some things.

Pat learned that when she played the three Meeks—Semeka, Chamique, and me—some remarkable things happened. She learned, as she substituted like crazy in the second half to try to not run up the score, that whatever new players she put in, there was a burst of new energy and scoring and tough defense.

She learned she didn't just have a collection of prima donnas.

She had a team.

Pat used a set of principles to build teamwork. She called them the Definite Dozen:

1. Respect Yourself and Others
2. Take Full Responsibility
3. Develop and Demonstrate Loyalty
4. Learn to Be a Great Communicator
5. Discipline Yourself So No One Else Has To
6. Make Hard Work Your Passion
7. Don't Just Work Hard, Work Smart
8. Put the Team Before Yourself
9. Make Winning an Attitude
10. Be a Competitor
11. Change Is a Must
12. Handle Success Like You Handle Failure

I don't remember if back then I truly understood the importance and deeper significance of these principles. But I know in my later career I have come on my own terms to embrace the ideas behind some of these principles, in particular those that talk about hard work.

It's one thing to talk about your passion and to think that's what you're going to excel in. I believe and say all the time that "it's good to pursue your passion." But just because it's your passion doesn't automatically mean you're going to be good at it.

If you look at the people who are really good at something—brilliant musicians, great writers, or those who play a mean game of basketball—you learn pretty quickly that, yes, they have talent in an area and, yes, they have a passion in that area. But they didn't get great just because of talent or passion. Lots of people have talent they never actually develop. Many pursue passions that never amount to much. Those people you admire are great in some area because they *work hard to be great*. They practice, they stay disciplined, and they doggedly push themselves to get better.

I have to say I kind of resent it when people make the comments that I'm "so talented" in basketball. Oh, I appreciate the compliment, but in saying that, there's a suggestion that it's all come naturally to me. That it's been easy. No. Not really. I'm good at what I do because I've worked hard, really hard, all my life to get good. I've practiced hard, disciplined myself, and pushed myself beyond measure.

If you want to achieve something in life, you have to work for it. Your talent will give you ability, and your passion will give you drive. But it's your hard work that will make you great.

And that's why, in November 1997, Pat Summitt was discovering something about our team that was really special. It was different, even from the other great teams she had coached. She was discovering, as we all were, that this team had a level of relentlessness about it, a drive to push harder and work harder, than any team she'd coached before. As she once wrote, "In the 1997–98 Lady Vols I finally met a group of players more driven than I am. They were harder on themselves than I ever could have been. That was clear the moment they stepped on campus."[1]

Yeah, we were driven. We worked hard. But we were about to face our toughest competition of the year in just our second game: with Louisiana Tech.

Tech was favored to win the game.

Their starting five were all veterans who had gotten the team into the tournament semifinals the year before. Amanda Wilson, Tamicha Jackson, Alisa Burras, LaQuan Stallworth, and Monica Maxwell had achieved significant honors already and would achieve more again later this season. This same lineup had beaten the Tennessee Lady Vols twice the year before.

We were a team composed mostly of underclassmen. Three of us would be playing in just our second college game. And our point guard, Ace, was iffy to play, still nursing a bum foot.

Their center, Burras, was a real threat. Not that she was taller than our centers, LaShonda Stephens or Tree, but she was muscled and solid. She would easily score in the double digits. Their point guard, Tamicha Jackson, was quick and elusive. Monica Maxwell, one of their forwards, could score buckets in a bunch real quick.

This being just our second game, we had no sense yet about what was at stake. Even if we lost, we'd have a measure of where we stood, as LA Tech was clearly the best competition we would likely see all year.

We knew how good they were. We just didn't know ourselves very well yet.

The game didn't start out well. Four minutes in, the Lady Techsters had scored eleven and we had only managed two baskets. Sure enough, Burras was having her way on the low post, while Maxwell sped around the perimeter feeding the ball to others.

Pat called a time-out. She sent in Ace to replace Kellie Jolly at point guard. It was a risky move, as Ace had yet to see any action in a college game and she was tentative on her injured foot. And, as it turned out, the move would cost the team later.

But the lineup change worked for the time being. We clawed back, although slowly, and we narrowed the gap by halftime, trailing by just a point, 36–35.

Pat lit into us at halftime. We were playing without confidence—uncertain, tentative. Pat used a phrase that proved to be a lightbulb turning on for us, not only for that game but for the season. "Let your defense be your offense," she said.

Sometimes you look for the one thing that will turn the game around—the magic phrase, the motivational speech, the daring strategy—and occasionally that works. But often it's not that one thing. Often it's simply hard work. Playing tough. Scratching and clawing out a win. Winning isn't always decisive or dramatic.

But sometimes it is.

In the second half, the Lady Techsters came out on fire. We held on as best we could, but after a few minutes we were down six points. Coach Summitt started trying some things.

She motioned Tree to get into the game. And in the next play, as LA Tech marched down the floor, Alisa Burras got the ball and drove big and hard toward the basket, stopping and shooting at point blank. *Here we go again*, we all thought.

But then, out of nowhere it seemed, Tree rose up, climbed some kind of invisible ladder, and swatted the shot away in a totally clean, legitimate block. It was like everyone in the arena paused at what they'd just seen. Then everyone on the Tennessee bench jumped up and all of Thompson-Boling erupted.

Next time down the court, Burras got the ball again and shot. And once again Tree rose up, climbed the air, and blocked the shot away. It was like in a matter of just halftime minutes, Tree had figured it out.

The Tennessee crowd went wild.

Coach then motioned Semeka into the game, followed by Ace on her aching foot. I was playing, and eventually Kyra Elzy as well.

With Tree playing lights out against Burras, the rest of us had a chance. And we went on a 12–0 run.

The Fab 4 had come to play.

At that point, just as Louisiana Tech was reeling, Pat brought back in her star, the best player in college basketball, Chamique Holdsclaw. Our knockout punch. And soon our lead rose to eight, then ten.

We went on to win the game, 75–61.

The Louisiana Tech game was the first of five games in nine days. A few of the games were against easier opponents, but one was top-ranked. It was no accident we were pushed hard to perform well in the midst of extreme fatigue.

Pat was counting on that.

She always planned the playing schedule year in, year out, and was known for intentionally creating a tough road through the season for her teams. She knew she coached the best teams, and she wanted us to be challenged at the highest level. What's more, she wasn't coaching for the regular season; she was coaching for the tournament and ultimately the championship, which meant a lot of games played in short periods of time.

The 1997–1998 schedule was one of the toughest she'd ever created.

After Louisiana Tech, we beat the Skyhawks at Tennessee-Martin, UT's sister school. They had named their basketball court after Pat Summitt, who had played there in her college career.

However, the game, although a handy win, proved to also be a loss for us. Semeka went up for a rebound and fell hard on her shoulder. On a subsequent play, she fought for another rebound and felt something in her arm. She grabbed it, and the pain was so great she couldn't stand up. The early prognosis was surgery and a two-month rehab, but the next morning doctors determined it was a minor separation and surgery wasn't needed.

We were already dealing with Ace's foot injury. As it turned out, Ace would miss five games.

We traveled to Vermont, winning there by forty points. But our big challenge was coming up. We would face Stanford just days later. Stanford was a tough foe and ranked eleventh.

We started slowly, and Stanford led us at halftime by a point. Our problem was defense.

Like, we weren't playing any.

Pat was steamed. At halftime she lit into us. "Is anyone going to guard anybody?" Her laser-blues were boring holes into every one of us.

Kyra Elzy came out the second half on a mission. She was draped all over their guards, and it disrupted the Stanford shooting. Kellie Jolly, playing full time without Ace in the game, was solid. Semeka played with her sore shoulder, and though frustrated by her shooting, still scored seventeen. The three of us Meeks would end the game with a total of sixty-two points. It was my best game of my college career so far. We wound up beating Stanford 88–70.

It's hard to know at what point during this becoming-remarkable season anyone had a sense of what was possible. We were good, we all knew, but any basketball season is long, prone to lulls, let-downs, adversity, and fatigue. Sometimes you just run into a really hot team. You're bound to lose some games along the way. The question is whether you can survive the season physically and mentally to be a force in the tournament. We were already dealing with injuries.

So while there was some sense that we were discovering who we could be as a team, and that was turning out to be something really special, there was always an awareness that we were just playing each game as it came, trying to learn life and basketball at the college level.

Pat tells the story of an encounter with an old friend and former coach of hers after that Stanford game. Billie Moore had had an illustrious career as a coach. Retired by then, she had been the coach of the U.S. Olympic team in 1976 and would be admitted to the Women's Basketball Hall of Fame a few years later.

She had attended the Stanford game and was evaluating our strengths and weaknesses as a team. When she and Pat connected after the game, she said, "Holy smokes, Pat." It was her way of saying that the talent we had was unbelievable.

Pat replied, "I know."

"There's only one team capable of beating Tennessee," Billie said.

"Who?"

"Tennessee."[2]

After the gauntlet of games that ran through the Thanksgiving holidays and into December, we had a week off.

On short breaks throughout college, I sometimes went to visit Dad in Chicago. Chicago was a nine-hour drive away—not a short trip, by any means, but closer than Duncanville, Texas. On longer holidays, I'd fly home to Texas, but often Chicago was the best option for the amount of time I had.

At that time my dad was the color analyst for the Chicago Bulls on WMAQ radio. It was a good time for him to do that—the Chicago Bulls, led by Michael Jordan, were in the midst of accomplishing their second "three-peat," having won the championship the previous two years and three championships in a row a few years before that. They'd go on to win it all that season—a remarkable six championships in eight years.

Of course, often Tauja would drive north from Champaign, Illinois, and we'd have time together. So during those years I had lots of reasons to go to Chicago.

Chamique tells the story of a time when we were both in Chicago on break. For some reason, I needed to drive down to Champaign to pick up a car from Tauja, then drive back to Knoxville. So the story goes, I called Chamique to ask her to drive with me. She agreed.

Because of the schedule, we had to drive back to Tennessee overnight. As Chamique tells it, she was at the wheel in the middle of the night. I was asleep. And at some point, she dozed off, the car drifting over toward the guard rail. The loud sound of the rumble strips jerked her awake, and she regained control of the car and brought us to a stop. We switched places and continued the trip home safely, aware that we had narrowly escaped becoming a tragic headline.

The only problem is, I don't remember any of that. Not saying that it didn't happen—it was vivid in Chamique's recollection, so it obviously did. But I think I must have been so exhausted from the trip to Chicago that I zoned out.

At times like that, it's good to know God is in control. It does make you think, though—how many dangers and accidents do we narrowly escape and never know it?

Tauja had been pursuing a basketball career of her own at the University of Illinois. Up next for Tennessee was the SEC/Big-Ten Challenge, which pitted us against the Fighting Illini.

The media pitched it as a battle between the Catchings Sisters. I never wanted that—my dream long ago was that the two of us would play *together*, not against each other. But here we were. I asked Coach Summitt to please not assign me to guard Tauja. Pat agreed but said, "You know at some point you may have to."

To make the event even more nerve-racking, both our parents were there in attendance. They didn't sit together, but they were both there. The media, of course, couldn't wait to get interviews with Dad talking about his daughters.

Somewhat lost in the media hype around the Catchings Sisters was the fact that Illinois was a strong team. They were nationally ranked fifth. We were sitting atop the rankings at number one, but this would be our toughest game since Louisiana Tech.

Illinois played a swarming, scrappy defense. The refs helped by calling a tight game. We hurt ourselves by taking bad shots, everything thudding off the back of the rim. We got into foul trouble early, and turned it over too many times. Chamique picked up two fouls within the first five minutes.

And, with a minute left in the first half, we were down 41 to 19.

Yes, it was that bad.

You face a psychological hurdle when your opponent doubles your score. You realize you have to play twice as good as them in the second half. You realize how unlikely it is that they will suddenly get that bad and you will suddenly get that good.

We expected to get a classic tirade from Pat at halftime, but I think she figured we'd gotten beaten badly enough already. She was instead calm and soft-spoken. She simply said we'd had bad luck in some of our shots not falling, and that the one thing we could/should do better was rebounding. That was it. She was unusually restrained.

We learned later that Pat had some pretty serious thoughts at halftime, thinking this would be our first loss and that the important thing at that point wasn't actually losing, but how we would handle the loss in the aftermath of the game. She would never give up, of course, but she was already coaching for the next game and the rest of the season.

One of our coaches, Al Brown, pulled me aside before we went out for the second half. He said, "The game is going to come to you. Just relax."

We came out in the second half playing tenacious defense. We still weren't scoring well, but by keeping the Illini from scoring and forcing them to turn over the ball, we stayed in the game. When Chamique eventually punched in two jumpers, the score was a more manageable 41 to 28.

But while we were playing Illinois even in the second half, we were still not outscoring them. Their lead remained at fourteen or sixteen points for the first six minutes.

Time was running out.

Kellie fed me the ball on the perimeter and I sank a three-pointer. We forced a turnover and Semeka got fouled, swishing two free throws. Another Illini turnover, and Kellie sized up a three and drilled it. Our smothering D forced yet another turnover.

In three minutes we'd cut their lead to five. In ten minutes, we'd forced *ten* turnovers.

At one point with about ten minutes left, Tauja was fed the ball on the open floor and went in for the fast break; I fouled her, keeping her from scoring. That was one of just a few times in the game when we found ourselves one-on-one with each other. Just like old times.

With nine minutes left, I was fouled and managed to make both free throws. With that we took the lead.

We never looked back. We continued our full-court press, and continued scoring off their turnovers.

Down by twenty-two in the first half, incredibly we won the game by ten points.

Later, my dad found both Tauja and me in the hallway outside the locker room. He told each of us we'd played great. We made it through the matchup of the Catchings Sisters. For Mom and Dad, it was a relief. I think it was for Tauja and me too.

One year old

First grade, in Milan, Italy

1995 state championship trophy

Senior year, 1997

Courtney McDaniel, Kristen "Ace" Clement, and Tamika with Coach Nell Fortner

Tamika with her mom, freshman year of college

Tamika with Coach Pat Summitt, freshman year

Tamika with her dad, 2004

Tauja, Tamika (wearing the gold medal from 2008 Olympics in Beijing), and Kenyon

Catch the Stars Youth Holiday Basketball Camp, 2007

Tamika, Kenyon, and Tauja, 2015

Playing hard

2015 Indiana Fever

So Tennessee made it past a swarming, smart Illinois team. Maybe more important, we'd overcome our biggest opponent in that first half.

Ourselves.

***

Pat Summitt now says of that game, that comeback, that it was then she realized she'd never coached a team "so combustible." She certainly knew there was a lot of basketball ahead, a lot of challenges for us to face, and so many things that could go wrong. But she'd coached for twenty-four years and was starting to see the real potential of the special group of players she had. She knew what she had in us was rare and special. Her question at that point was whether we'd play to our potential. So far, when we did, we were astonishing. And when we didn't, we were ordinary, and maybe worse.[3]

Me, I was just enjoying playing basketball and being in college with my friends. I'd had a lot of success on the teams I'd played for in high school, and I expected to win in college as well. Not that a loss would have thrown me into depression, but I was playing with the best and for the best, and it was an invigorating time for me to play at such a high level.

Dorm life was fun. When the team wasn't traveling, we were in classes, studying hard. Pat insisted on high academic performance from all of us. So we worked hard that way too.

When we had a chance to blow off some steam, the Fab 4 would get together in the dorm and sing karaoke or just hang. Seeing some of my teammates turn on a popular song and let it all out singing and dancing to it was hilarious. Of all people, Chamique was one of the best. I still remember her version of "Ball and Chain": "Sitting at the window, honey, looking out at the rain. . . ." She absolutely nailed Janis Joplin. It was just so Mique—over the top. We'd laugh and laugh.

The week before Christmas found us in Anchorage, Alaska, for the Northern Lights Invitational. It was cold compared to Knoxville, but we got to go sledding, which was a treat. We'd face three opponents in three days. Again, this was Pat's designed schedule, to test our stamina now in preparation for the tournament later. We defeated Akron, Texas A&M, and Wisconsin in quick succession. Wisconsin was nationally ranked, but it didn't seem to show—we beat them by twenty-one points.

This was the time that our shooting caught fire. All three of us Meeks were named to the All-Tournament team.

After the first half of the regular season, at the Christmas break, we were 13–0. We were regularly beating teams by twenty points, sometimes thirty.

And, to the dismay of opponents, our play was getting better. We were still learning how to play together.

Back in 1995, Pat Summitt and the coach of the University of Connecticut, Geno Auriemma, had this crazy idea to schedule games against each other. UConn was a top women's basketball program, winning it all that year. What's more, the two coaches were larger-than-life personalities, each of them legends already, shrewd and smart—and depending on which college you were talking to, the other one nothing less than ruthless. Games played against each other took on the drama and theater of gladiator fights.

We faced UConn, ranked number three, on January 3, 1998.

UConn had the edge in the head-to-head—4–3 since 1995. We were on a tear. They wanted nothing more than to derail our march to the tournament and create the first blemish on our perfect season.

Thompson-Boling Arena was filled to the brim, a record crowd not just for Tennessee but for all of women's college basketball. They had to turn away some eight hundred people at the doors because it was already standing room only. The arena was loud and electric, a frenzied mass of fans eager to watch the battle of the coaches—Pat versus Geno.

Just two minutes into the game, Nykesha Sales took the ball at the top of the key. Chamique was right there and blanketed Nykesha with tight defense. A minute later Nykesha took a wild shot from well beyond the perimeter, an air ball that went out of bounds. It would be a long game, of course, but we all felt better seeing Mique contain Nykesha right off the bat.

I knew I needed to do more than my usual part. With Mique expending so much energy on defense, she might not have so much in the tank for offense. Our plan was to use her as a decoy on offense. In the first sequence of plays, we ran the triple post,[4] with Chamique sliding down toward the basket. UConn players would sag down toward her, leaving me open on the outside.

I came out hot. I was able to score seven points in the first two minutes. We were up 10–0 after the first three minutes of the game.

But we knew they'd roar back, and they did. In another four minutes they cut our lead to one. We padded that by the end of the first quarter, when we were up by six.

That was another unique aspect of that particular game. It was played in quarters. Usually college basketball was played in two 20-minute halves. The pros play four 10-minute quarters. This game was a four-quarter experiment. (I'm not sure the experiment made much difference to anyone.)

We made it a fast-break game, with what was becoming our patented swarming defense and racing offense. We led by as many as seventeen in the first half.

Mique held Nykesha Sales to six points.

The second half played according to the same script, although UConn came out in a frenzied push. Halfway through the third quarter, they cut our lead to just one point. But once again we took hold of the game, rebuilt the lead, and then ran away with the game.

The great rivalry game ended with us on top—a score of 84–69.

Later, Semeka Randall would get caught in a controversy. She was asked by a reporter if the crowd had been a factor in the game. She said, "Yeah, I think Connecticut just about ran off the floor, they were so scared."

Well, that didn't go over well with the state of Connecticut. Her quote was taken out of context, but UConn coach Geno Auriemma would take offense and say some negative things of his own back at Semeka and us. It would be in another game in another year that we would play UConn on their home court, and Semeka would get booed loudly. As a result, she earned the nickname "Boo." Ever after, she wore that nickname proudly.

The controversy only fueled a great rivalry that would last for the next ten years. It also revved up new interest in women's college basketball. The women's game was gaining fans and helping fuel the new WNBA professional league spawned by the NBA.

That Pat Summitt and Geno Auriemma were crazy, all right. Crazy like foxes.

In February, we faced a stretch of five games in ten days. Old Dominion was first up on the fourth, then Mississippi State, Memphis, and Auburn in quick succession. None of them were close games, though Old Dominion was ranked third in the nation at the time of that game. Winning big or not, we still played the minutes. Four of the five games were on the road, which always takes more out of you.

Our last game would be against an SEC foe and our arch-rival in the state of Tennessee, the Vanderbilt Lady Commodores. And we were exhausted.

This was another one of the scheduling gauntlets Pat Summitt intentionally created for her teams. She addressed this in the locker room before the Vandy game. "I'm to blame for this schedule," she told us all. "I did it by design. So why would I do that?"

I spoke up. "To see if we can handle it."

"Correct," she said.

Even so, I wondered if, at certain points of this season as our record continued to build, Pat was starting to regret her scheduling strategy, realizing that we were now making history and seeing that ominous fifth game in ten days looming as a trap game for a team of exhausted college players.

But that last game of those ten days wasn't a trap game. We'd already played Vandy once, and won, but they were nationally ranked and always a threat. We knew it wasn't an automatic. We wouldn't get trapped because we were taking the game for granted as a win, but we could lose outright. They were very good.

Sure enough, we came out flat. We were, for one of very few times that season, actually slow. Vandy jumped out to a 16–7 lead. We gave up more turnovers (8) than we scored points. It was pretty ugly.

Pat called a time-out. She knew our performance was due to fatigue—and she was tired too—but she made it clear we had to take care of the ball. She got us focused not on the whole game or on the score, but on each possession of the ball. If we focused on making each possession count, we'd be okay.

In the last ten minutes before halftime, we came out on fire. Pat had the three of us Meeks in the game at that point, and we began to score, almost at will. We went on a 17–0 run over the next six minutes, leading at halftime by nine.

Pat challenged us not to ease up, not to let Vandy back into the game. And we complied, keeping them quiet in the second half and scoring nearly twice as many points as we had in the first half. We won 91–60, a score that doesn't reflect how tough the game really was for us.

Later, Pat would write about that game. It was then she began consciously to allow a dangerous thought, one she'd banned from her mind much of the season. *Maybe, just maybe, this team might go undefeated.*[5]

The Vandy win gave us a record of 29–0. We had one more regular season game, and then the SEC tournament before the national tournament.

We faced LSU in the last game of the season. Our only concern was our own health. Everyone was banged up. To make things worse, I went hard to the basket in practice, banged heads with one of our practice guys, and broke my nose. Assistant Coach Holly Warlick was the first to come to my side and apparently was almost unable to look at me because my face was such a mess. There was blood everywhere, I was in great pain, and someone said it looked like my nose had moved some inches along my face and repositioned itself under my eye.

It would require minor surgery and a doctor would have to pop my nose back into place. But after some swelling went down, it wasn't so bad.

Really, it wasn't.

I remember two things about the LSU game.

One. We were at home, which was a good thing, because we needed the energy of the crowd. They were so proud of us, a team on the verge of history. With a win that night, we'd finish the regular season 30–0.

Two. It was a game when the Fab 4—the freshmen—lit up the court. Coach Summitt left the four of us on the court for more minutes than usual, and we freshmen—just the freshmen—wound up scoring some sixty-five points among us.

We won going away, but I was especially happy because my roommate Ace, who had struggled all season, had a strong game. Not only had she had the foot injury at the start of the season, one which became a nagging injury for a long time, but Pat had been especially tough on her along the way. Coach challenged Ace hard and often, and while I think some of that might have been needed, it was still hard on Ace. Sometimes too hard. But now Ace was coming into her own. Maybe just at the right time.

Perhaps had we not been so tired at that point, it might have gone to our heads. The media were starting to write about us. The articles started to ask if we were the best team of all time.

I don't know if that was sinking in for anybody on the team. For one thing, there was a lot of basketball left. For another thing, Pat wouldn't let it, even though she knew she was at the helm of something special.

As for me, I didn't know if we were the best of all time. It didn't matter.

I just loved playing the game.

10

CHAMPIONS

"Tamika, I want you to know and believe that no one in America can stop you . . ."

Pat Summitt

The SEC conference regional was held at the end of February, and we played three more games. Since we had a perfect record, and since we'd played all these same teams in our conference at least once before, there wasn't much to worry about in the SEC regional—although twentieth-ranked Alabama played us tight in the final. And since so many of our games had been blowouts, you might think it was good for us to play in a closely contested game right before the tournament. But we simply played slow and were lethargic on the boards. What's more, Alabama may have given the rest of the country some idea about how to beat us—slow us down with tight, physical play. Whatever. We made our foul shots down the stretch and won by four. With the SEC conference wins, our record was an incredible 33–0. Not that we needed to talk up that record any, but two things were sometimes overlooked. One was that we had reached that record by playing what was considered one of the toughest schedules in women's college basketball that year. The other was that we were a team that played the majority of our underclassmen; we regularly went up against teams that started three or more seniors, players with extensive court experience.

Chalk it up to the freshman talent; give a nod to Pat for awesome coaching; make a bow toward Mique, whom Nancy Lieberman was calling the best player in women's basketball. No matter how you looked at it, our 33–0 record was remarkable.

A media frenzy swirled around the team the week before the tournament brackets were announced. A documentary film (about the previous year's team) premiered. Pat's new book—*Reach for the Summit*—strategically launched in early March. I remember that some of us, while shopping at the mall, were stopped for autographs. We were living the life, and I remember thinking to myself, *If this is how it's going to be for the next four years, I don't want it to ever end.* Our hard work was paying off, and through all the blood, pain, and fight this team had given, we were being rewarded both on and off the court. These moments were truly a dream come true.

We had about a week and a half between the last regular season game and the first game of the NCAA tournament. That allowed us to catch up on studies, take exams, and most importantly—do laundry.

When the brackets were announced, we were the number one seed in the Mideast region. We'd play Liberty in the first round. Liberty also boasted an undefeated season, albeit in a less competitive conference. Still, they featured a couple of star players—twins—Sarah and Sharon Wilkerson, guards who excelled at outside shooting. They had been instrumental in rejuvenating the basketball program at the small Christian college founded by Jerry Falwell.

The Road to the Final Four would start with our first two games in Thompson-Boling, which was a customary venue for one of the regions in the tournament. The regional rounds would be hosted in Nashville. And, ultimately, the Final Four would be played in Kansas City.

Coach practiced us during the break, though practices were light. There was nothing new we needed to learn at this point. Mostly we needed to rest, stay healthy, and keep in shape. One of the team rituals before the NCAA tourney was to watch a highlight video that had been prepared for us. It was invigorating to watch it, and also in a way humbling. It showed us how good we could be. But we also knew we sometimes didn't play to that level.

Another pretourney ritual Pat had was writing each of us personal notes, something specific about each one of us. Encouragement. I know she was trying to bolster our confidence and relieve any jitters we each might have, but it was also genuine, how she really felt. It meant a lot. Her note to me read, "Dear Tamika, I want you to know and believe that no one in America can stop you . . ."

The game with Liberty wasn't close; most number one to number sixteen matchups aren't. Both Chamique and I wound up with double-doubles.

We won, getting us one step closer to our ultimate goal—the championship.

The bracket system of NCAA basketball is set up to run four regional competitions simultaneously, each region seeded with sixteen teams—sixty-four teams overall. Every game is single-elimination—you lose, you're done. Four teams in each region survive—known as the Sweet Sixteen. Winners of those games advance to the Elite Eight. The survivors of those games head to the Final Four. And the final two teams play for the championship. In short, win six games and you're the champions.

The thing is, no matter how good you are—even if you're 34–0—there's a chance that something will sabotage you along the way. Injury, disciplinary problems, fatigue, a slow start to a game, fouling trouble—*something* can take any team out before the end of that sixth game.

We didn't worry about the level of our play. We believed we could beat anybody. And we had beaten everybody. What we worried about were these other random elements that might damage us before we had the chance. I know Pat worried about that too. A lot.

We faced Western Kentucky next. Semeka picked up two quick fouls, and that took her out of the game until later. But Ace came in midway through the first half and scored five points quickly, and that put us up by seven. Still, it was a seesaw game until the end, when we pulled away. We won 82–62. Mique had a monster night with thirty-four points.

The win got us into the Sweet Sixteen and a trip to Nashville.

It was customary for the four teams that landed in the regional to attend a banquet the night before the games began. A lot of us in the final sixteen teams knew each other from playing each other in high school or the Junior Nationals, so it was a time to talk, catch up, renew old friendships. It was also a time for some trash talk.

Some of the Rutgers players cornered Chamique and Semeka and spoke about how overrated we were. Specifically they called out Semeka and told her directly that she was *really* overrated. It was all competitive spirit, and Semeka just smiled, but it was talk that kind of got to her down inside.

Rutgers was a young team like us, also with four freshmen on the squad. They'd played a tough schedule all year, and though young, they were seasoned. They had a lot of confidence and swagger. Their freshman guard Natasha Pointer was dangerous, and they had a bunch of scorers. We could have our hands full.

They were ready for us. They closely matched us through the first half. We kept Pointer in check, but Tomora Young, a junior and quite a sharpshooter, went off, scoring whenever they needed it. With a few minutes left, Rutgers was within two.

But Semeka, with swarming energy that disrupted the Scarlet Knights, propelled us to a late surge, and we ended the half up by eight.

The second half was no contest. We quickly built a lead of sixteen points, and Rutgers never got close. We won 92–60, once again our defensive pressure wearing down the other team in the late going. Semeka was the star of the game by all accounts, scoring a double-double with seventeen points, thirteen rebounds, and four steals.

We were guessing that after Semeka's performance, nobody could think—or say—she was overrated.

We had to wait to see who our next opponent would be. The game to decide that was between Illinois and North Carolina.

Tauja.

Illinois was the third seed in the Mideast region, and she and I had known we could wind up facing each other. The Illini had already beaten Wisconsin-Green Bay and UC Santa Barbara to get to the Sweet Sixteen. Now they would go up against a fast, physical North Carolina team.

If they advanced, it would be Tennessee versus Illinois. Tamika versus Tauja once again. It was nerve-racking to me, wishing on the one hand for Tauja and Illinois to win, but dreading the thought of us playing each other again. Mom and Dad were there to watch us both. I sat with Mom, courtside, to watch Tauja play.

Tauja played great, pulling down fourteen rebounds while pouring in sixteen points. It was a close game, but ultimately North Carolina prevailed.

There would be no Catchings Sisters matchup. On the one hand I wanted to see my sister advance, but on the other hand I wanted to avoid a sibling conflict. Facing North Carolina instead of Illinois would keep this tournament from being another media frenzy for me. I didn't want the distraction.

Two days later we played North Carolina in the Elite Eight. Every game now was a little scary because the level of competition was so high. After such a perfect season, losing would be devastating. North Carolina was ranked number seven, a strong team, certainly, but we had beaten better teams all year.

Little did we know, as we walked into Vanderbilt's Memorial Stadium, that this would be our toughest game of the season.

The Tar Heels came out running.

They were a dangerous team for us because they were so much *like* us. We had the reputation for creating a new kind of women's basketball—fast and physical. The *New York Times* would write, "Beyond Tennessee's statistical dominance lies an aggressive, attacking style that has redefined the women's game and offered the sharpest departure to date from the stationary days when women relied mostly on set shots."

But here it was North Carolina coming out on the attack. On the very first play, their guard Nikki Teasley fed the ball to their shooter, senior Tracy Reid, for a basket. It was an omen of what was to come.

It was close through the first half. With seven minutes to go, the score was tied, 21–21.

We weren't used to this relentless style being played *against* us. They were outrunning us, up and down the court. They were playing loose, and we were tensing up. Because of the tension, our shots weren't falling.

During halftime, Pat lit into us for our poor defense. All year, that had been her fallback position. When nothing else is working, play defense. And she admonished us, "Whatever you do, don't let them start out the second half like they did the first half. Don't let them go on a run."

Coming out the second half, North Carolina went on a run, 7–0.

We were getting beat badly. Our shots weren't falling. They were shooting 64 percent. Lights out. Pat and the coaches had tried everything. They were exasperated. And exhausted. And starting to feel hopeless.

With seven minutes left in the second half, we were down by twelve. And that sounded better than it felt. In this game, twelve points was a mountain to climb.

We took a time-out, and as we sauntered over to the bench, it was Kellie Jolly who took over.

She grabbed Pat's footstool, slammed it down, and looked each of us in the eyes while yelling at us in the middle of the huddle. Pat watched from a distance. "Listen to me. We've got to run the floor," she yelled. "We've got to run. We've got to go. We've got to go. *Now.*"

Then Kyra stepped in. "Are we going to Kansas City?"

She repeated it. "Are we going to Kansas City?"

No one answered.

She repeated it again. And again. And again.

Finally, Tree—quiet, silent Tree—said calmly, finding something deep inside herself. "Yes. We're gonna go to Kansas City."

"Okay, then," Kyra said. "We're going. Let's go!"

Ace inbounded the ball, finding Tree, who promptly eluded her defender and drove to the basket for a layup. And she was fouled. She sank the free throw, and it was as if this quiet giant had emerged for the special moment. Tree changed the feel of the game for us.

At the other end, we pressed on defense. Mique grabbed a rebound, was fouled, and sank both her free throws. North

Carolina raced to the other end, and Tracy Reid lined up for a shot that had been falling all night for her. But once again, there was Tree, who rose up out of nowhere. Racing to our basket, I was fed the ball, and I shot from three-point land. I missed, but Tree (who else?) grabbed the rebound and banked it into the basket.

In less than a minute we'd scored seven points. The Tar Heels' lead was down to five.

Now it was Ace's moment. She raced the ball along the baseline. North Carolina sagged in to defend against her. She then found me under the basket, zipped the ball to me unguarded, and I scored. On the other end, Mique grabbed a rebound, and we were off to the races again. Fouled, Mique sank both free throws.

Suddenly it was a tie game.

With twenty-one seconds left to go we were up—but by just two. North Carolina started fouling. Pat had just gotten Kellie in—our best free throw shooter. Sure enough, she got fouled—and sank both free throws.

With five seconds to go the Tar Heels' Teasley fired a three from long range.

It missed.

The game was over. And we'd narrowly escaped disaster. We'd made it to the Final Four. We were on our way to Kansas City.

And we were about to make history.

We faced Arkansas in our semifinal and won by nearly thirty. The winner of the other semi was Louisiana Tech. In the championship game, we would play the team we faced in the second week of the season. Tech had lost only three games all year. They would be formidable.

Despite our win, I was disappointed with myself. I'd had a bad game, and I knew it.

It was Coach Brown who came to me after the Arkansas game. I knew he wasn't happy with me, either, but all he said was to find him later to watch some tape.

Coach Brown and I had had a special relationship. The assistant coaches on the team—Mickie DeMoss, Holly Warlick, and Al Brown—had several important responsibilities. One was basketball coaching, of course—leading team practices and drills, pointing out problems in form and execution, and advising players on technique.

Another responsibility was, quite frankly, keeping Pat Summitt in check. Calming her down when she was furious and helping her keep a balanced perspective on the problems of the team. And Pat listened to them. They had good rapport.

A third thing the coaches did was to counsel and motivate individual players. Each coach took on several players to come alongside personally during the season. They each had their assignments. When one of us was dealing with a personal problem, was frustrated with her game, or was dealing with a relationship issue, a coach was usually there in a personal way.

Al Brown had taken me on. We had developed a good connection because he knew how to challenge and motivate me. I liked him because he was just straight-up honest with me. He knew how competitive I was. If he told me I couldn't do something, I would do it. And he knew that's exactly what I would do.

When Coach Brown opened his hotel room (aka the film room) later that night, I could tell he had probably watched the game a few times and had been waiting for me so we could watch together. Immediately I admitted that I kind of bailed out in that game. "I played terrible," I said.

"Yeah, you did," he replied, nodding.

It made me angry that he was agreeing with me so quickly. He didn't stop there. "You know who we're playing next," he said. "Louisiana Tech."

I nodded.

"Amanda Wilson," he said. He let her name hang in the air for effect. Amanda Wilson was Tech's hot-scoring forward, an All-American, and later to be drafted into the WNBA.

He went on. "She'll probably have about thirty points and fifteen rebounds. A half-dozen assists." Coach Brown paused. "And you, I'm thinking you might not even score. She's that good."

My heart started beating fast. I was mad about him talking to me like that. I was ready to argue with him, but I bit my tongue.

"If you play like you played today," he warned, "she's gonna eat you alive."

And that I couldn't disagree with.

The next day, preceding the championship game, we were the focus of extraordinary media attention. Every year the final two teams get some of that, but we were Pat Summitt's team, and she was going for her third straight championship. No one on the team wanted to use the phrase "three-peat" for fear of jinxing anything, but that didn't stop the media from using it.

The night before the championship game, we had to attend another banquet. Both Chamique and I had been named to the Kodak All-American Team. My teammates were there, as were Coach Summitt, Mickie DeMoss, and the other coaches. Both Mom and Dad took pictures of me as I stood on the stage. It was truly an honor.

The team piled back onto the bus afterward to go back to the hotel. We were all tired and maybe uptight about the game to come. The bus was quiet. Mile after mile, the bus rumbled down the road.

Suddenly, out of the silence, a voice started singing.

It was Assistant Coach Mickie DeMoss. She was softly voicing the lyrics and melody of the old hymn "Love Lifted Me":

> I was sinking deep in sin, far from the peaceful
>   shore,
> Very deeply stained within, sinking to rise no more,
> But the Master of the sea, heard my despairing cry,
> From the waters lifted me, now safe am I.
> Love lifted me! Love lifted me!
> When nothing else could help Love lifted me!

As Mickie sang through the first verse, others started to join in. When Mickie forgot some lyrics from the second verse, Kellie Jolly chimed in. She knew the hymn by heart. Then others of us sang as well, perhaps remembering a past Sunday at church or gospel service or an evening hymn-sing from when we were children.

We were remembering the warm assurance of a childhood faith, one that was perhaps more nostalgic and distant than it should have been.

In the national broadcast, ESPN announcer Mike Patrick introduced the game: "Pat Summitt won her first NCAA title at Tennessee. Tonight, in the most dominating run in the history of the women's game, she goes for number six. Heading the list of her superstar weapons—Chamique Holdsclaw, national player of the year and regarded by many as the best college player ever. When Summitt welcomed the best freshman class in Tennessee history, the stage was set for greatness. The depth of their talent, quickness, and intensity has produced thirty-eight consecutive wins by an incredible average of over thirty points a game. And, tonight, a chance to make history."[1]

Louisiana Tech pulled down the tipoff and immediately scored, setting the tempo. A minute later, Semeka outhustled the Tech player for a rebound, and then drove it fast up the floor, pulling up, and draining a jumper. Shortly after, Kellie Jolly grabbed a rebound and raced to the basket, at the last minute feeding it back to me. I scored.

After we grabbed another rebound, Chamique scored on a layup. We were up by six.

Like many other teams we'd played, LA Tech seemed to expect that once we had grabbed a rebound we'd stop, collect ourselves, and calmly walk the ball back to our end. Not tonight. Pat wanted us to play fast, and every rebound we grabbed was followed by a sprint the other way.

In one sequence, I ran the ball down to the baseline, Chamique trailed me, and I fed it to her for a layup. In the next sequence, Chamique returned the favor—as she was contested for the ball off to the side of the basket, she came up with it and shot it over the rim to me on the other side, where I grabbed it and popped it in for two. It was like playing volleyball.

For the next few minutes, we may have played the best basketball we'd played all year. Our defense was relentless, forcing steals, grabbing rebounds. We were flying up and down the court, passing the ball back and forth, sometimes scoring without the ball ever hitting the floor.

By halftime, we'd scored fifty-five points—more points in a half than had ever before been scored in college basketball.

Back in the locker room, despite our record-setting performance, Pat was still coaching. Worried about a letdown, she sounded the alarm against letting Louisiana Tech back in it. A quick run at the start of the second half, and they could perhaps get some confidence. After all, that's what we had done in the North Carolina game.

Sure enough, LA Tech scored the first seven points of the second half. Pat called a quick time-out and started yelling at us. "Are you going to let them back in it? Or are you going to play some defense?"

I was thinking, *We're the best team who just finished playing the best half of all time. And yet we're getting yelled at in this game too.* I still didn't like getting yelled at.

Coming back out, I grabbed a rebound and spotted Ace at the other end. I passed long to her, and she made a layup. Mique dropped a jumper in, and then I stole the ball and ran it the length of the floor for a layup. We had weathered the initial storm.

But Louisiana Tech wouldn't go away. At the twelve-minute mark they scored from three-point land, then on a foul, retained the ball and made another basket. Five points in one trip down the floor.

On our next possession, Kellie nailed a three from far out to answer. And then, after we got the rebound on the other end, Kellie got the ball again and lined up from way, way out, and dropped another three-pointer.

Everything they did to climb back into the game, we responded to.

With two minutes left, we were up by eighteen. Pat started substituting to allow some of the other players on the team to have an appearance in the game. Kyra Elzy, who had a torn ACL early in the year and didn't see much playing time, got in. Laurie Milligan, our lone senior, had appeared in the previous three seasons' final championship games. This year she'd had knee surgery. Pat made sure she got into this championship game too, setting a record. Coach Pat took care of her players. She took care of her "family."

At the end, we won, and we won big, 93–75.

We won the NCAA championship.

The crowd, so many of them Tennessee fans, erupted. Pat smiled big. You could see the pressure of the season roll off her shoulders. I saw Coach Brown out of the corner of my eye. Amanda Wilson had finished with just four points and five rebounds. That was a team effort, of course, but I'd kind of made sure of it.

Coach Brown came up to me with a big grin on his face. "I'm proud of you," he said.

I looked at him and it dawned on me. "You said all that on purpose, didn't you? I can't believe you did that!"

He just laughed. He knew he'd motivated me to have one of my best games ever.

Hugs and congratulations were exchanged all around. The media took over on the court, announcing the players and coaches and making presentations. Chamique won player of the game, and rightly so.

It was a huge accomplishment for Pat. Her third NCAA championship in a row. Never been done before in the modern era. All year, our line had been "Forget about history." We weren't ever playing under the burden of winning number three. We were just intent on winning this season and being the best team we could be. But now that we had done it, it was time to remember history.

Three championship wins in a row for Pat Summitt. Remarkable.

It was a long endurance race for our team, but we'd established ourselves as one of the premiere women's college teams of all time. We went 39–0, a record. We'd played one of the toughest schedules, including a dozen nationally ranked teams. And we'd done it with a squad of four freshmen, all of us still finding ourselves as college students, young women, and basketball players.

At the time I didn't fully understand what the significance of this was for the team or for me. Our championship run had drawn the attention of the nation. It had raised the level of recognition for women's basketball. As one of the commentators said after the game, "Everywhere you go, the excitement of this perfect team gets everyone involved. People want to talk about Tennessee. People are talking about women's basketball, women's college basketball. It's reached a new level of excitement."

I'd come into Tennessee for the purpose of being with the best players and playing for the best coach. Already, in one glorious season, we had become the best in the sport.

11

GOD

I can do all things through Christ who strengthens me.

Philippians 4:13 NKJV

We came back to school after a summer that, for each of us, was a kind of celebrity tour in our hometowns.

Since the championship, the Lady Vols had become a national treasure, and the focus on us was intense. Fortunately, a lot of this attention was absorbed by Pat, who rightly deserved it, yet felt out of place in it. The famous photographer Annie Leibovitz came to photograph her. The magazine *GQ* did a big feature article, and Pat didn't know the magazine, referring to it as "QT." Coach, along with Mique and Kellie Jolly, appeared on *The Rosie O'Donnell Show*.

Later Chamique would label us "the Beatles of basketball."

Commentators made much of the fact that the following year Tennessee was not losing any of its top starters to graduation. Mique and Kellie Jolly would be seniors, LaShonda Stephens and Niya Butts would be juniors. And then we Fab 4, along with Kyra Elzy, would be returning as sophomores. "The Meeks" would be together another year.

It was kind of foreordained that we would be the favorite to win it all once again. We would see.

Knoxville is gorgeous in the fall. The colors are brilliant and deep, a mosaic of autumn dotted all over the hills and mountains. A half-hour drive puts you in the middle of the Smoky Mountains near Gatlinburg. Just another ninety minutes away is Asheville, North Carolina. The best times for fall color in the area were the last two weeks of October. We were well into practices then, but not yet into the tough schedule of real games. I loved when I had time to get away and just drive. Almost like being able to escape to my own "colorful" world where no one could find me.

I think sometimes people see me as a driven, no-nonsense person, and maybe they miss the deeper things inside me. I don't know, but maybe because of my hearing loss, through the years the world outside has been more distant for me than for other people, and maybe I've developed more of a private, inner life instead. I think deeply, feel deeply, but those things don't often come out visibly to other people.

When I could get away from basketball and classes, most of the time I would drive out to a small lake about twenty minutes from campus. It was a special place to me, a place apart, so far from everyone, quiet and hushed except for the music of nature. There, I would find my way to one of my private spots and sit, sometimes for hours, just looking across the water and thinking and sometimes praying. I would often write my ideas and thoughts, hurts and dreams in a notebook. I'd write about my life, about what was going on, about other people. Eventually my deepest feelings would rush out, often in the form of poetry.

I keep a lot bottled up inside myself. That probably goes back to my childhood, I know. Those feelings are often stuffed down inside, but they do come out eventually, and often onto the pages of my notebooks.

Pat Summitt was not only a disciplinarian on the court; she was one off the court too. It mattered that her players did well in college. She checked on how each of us was doing in classes and emphasized the importance of studying hard and doing well.

Pat never needed to worry about me academically. I loved school. I loved learning. Still do. I love discovering new things, learning about new areas of knowledge. Sure, sometimes a subject doesn't interest me, and I'll move on from that. But many of my classes were interesting, and I found that in most subjects, I enjoyed my studies. In many areas of life, I just love to *learn*.

My major was in sports management. I also had a minor in business. I've always been interested in how competitive sports works. The business of it. I've always been fascinated by the process of running a team, finding talent, bringing in people to an organization, and making different pieces fit.

Even back then, as a sophomore at Tennessee, I watched Pat Summitt, not just as a basketball coach but as a woman who created an organization of talent and standards that succeeded at the highest levels. Watching her, I became interested in how you build a team, how you design an organization for success.

Frankly, though we were a team of great talent, if we'd had another coach and another organization, I don't know if we'd have made it 39–0 and be wearing NCAA Championship rings. Certainly there was something in Pat's soul and passion that got us there, but also there was a lot of smart, strategic team- and organization-building. I wanted to learn that.

I wanted someday to *do* that.

We came out of the gate in the fall of 1999 with an exhibition game against a team from Sweden. We won by forty points, and then went on to play Portland, whom we also beat handily.

I don't know, maybe we had started to take everything for granted. The coaches didn't have a good feeling going into the next game against Purdue. Neither did I. We just weren't *together.* Over the summer, Pat had gotten two new recruits, the six five Michelle Snow, a center who could dunk the ball, and Shalon Pillow, a potential dynamo on the court. But teams always incorporate new freshmen without too much disruption—and Pat had made it work just fine with the Fab 4 of us freshmen the year before. Playing together wasn't our only problem.

Our other problem was complacency, a lack of passion . . . no sense of urgency.

Purdue beat us 78–68.

Later, Pat would say it was the best thing that could happen to us. The loss served as a reminder that we weren't invincible. A caution that we needed to work for what we wanted to achieve. This loss could motivate us for the rest of the season.

Maybe, but I didn't like it. *I hate to lose.*

I think it was November 1999 when I was driving around town and passed a billboard that attracted my attention. It read, "Who's Your Daddy?"

It was an ad for a guest speaker at a church, the sermon title for Wednesday Night Bible Study.

I thought this was an extremely appropriate message for me and my dormmates to hear. We were all at different points in our relationship with our fathers, and I still had my struggles because of my parents' divorce. That sermon seemed targeted right at us.[1]

I went back to the dorm and told the girls about it. "Maybe we should check it out." They all agreed. And so we went to church that Wednesday.

A lot of African Americans grow up in church. We have an upbringing that teaches us about God and Jesus. In a way it's real to us as kids, but in another way we don't really understand how important it is to life. And once we get away from home, we get away from church, and we get away from God.

The guest speaker was Ken Freeman, and he was on the stage at Grace Baptist Church in Knoxville. His sermon was so powerful. One of his statements was, "No matter where you are, even though your earthly father may not be with you, your heavenly Father is always there." For the four of us sitting there, the message became very personal. For one thing, it was a call for some of us to return to God. For another thing, it soothed a deep hurt for us to realize that God himself could fill the hole in our souls left by the daddies in our lives who had been absent at times.

For me, and I think for others, it was like we heard God saying, "Where have you been? You've let basketball dominate your life, haven't you? How about some time for me, your Father in heaven? I'm here to fill that hole in your life."

It was an *aha* moment, deeply emotional, and personally motivating to us all. After the sermon, there was an altar call. It didn't take long for us to feel that call. Every one of the four of us went down front for prayer and to give our lives *back* to Christy.

That was the night I believe I truly got saved, the night I made a decision to dedicate my life to him.

I realized that I'd made basketball the most important thing in my life. I knew deep down that I needed God to be in charge. This changed my perspective and my life, although I'd need to be reminded again and again how I'd taken the ball of my life, run with it on my own, and taken my own shots for my own glory. I knew I needed to acknowledge that God was the one truly in control. Not easy for a stubborn girl from Duncanville, Texas. But I let go of my life.

And let God into my life.

After the Purdue loss that year, we finally pulled it together. We won our next twenty-four games, including a win over archrival UConn in Connecticut in early January.

You'd think that was a good thing.

But we faced injuries along the way. Tree went down in the UCLA game, hyperextending her knee, and she wasn't the same for the rest of the season. And even though we were winning, something was off, I could tell. We weren't winning as impressively as we had the year before.

We lost again. End of the season, right before the SEC tournament, against Louisiana State University by three points. As in the earlier loss, we weren't playing together. It was a lot of one-on-one, individuals trying to do it all. I was probably part of the problem.

We went on to win the SEC tournament, which landed us at 28–2 for the season. Yes, it's a terrific record, but in a way it wasn't about the record of wins and losses. We weren't really competing against the rest of the country. We were competing against ourselves. Were we playing as good as we possibly could? The answer was no.

I think that's the story of life as well. Am I as an individual doing all I can do with what God has given me? We aren't competing against the people around us. It doesn't matter if we get the gold ring at the end of the season. It matters only if we've done the work and performed at the level God has given us opportunity to attain.

We play for an audience of one—God. Or at least we should.

We entered the NCAA tournament as favorites to win a fourth straight championship. Our first game against sixteenth seed Appalachian State was a blowout—we won by nearly sixty points. Number one seeds versus number sixteen seeds sometimes don't seem fair, but plenty of sixteenth-seeded Cinderella teams win because the top-ranked teams fall asleep on the court. Our path through the tournament went through Boston College and Virginia Tech. Again, no problem for us. Some said we were playing at a WNBA level. We landed in the regional against Duke in Greensboro. The winner would go to the Final Four in San Jose. Duke is usually a formidable team, and yet when we had played them earlier in the season, we won by fourteen. So the question was, would we come with our A-game?

After the first six minutes, the score was 8–6, Duke ahead. I felt like we came out strong enough, contesting shots and playing good defense, but our shots just weren't falling.

At the half, Duke led by eleven points. Chamique had scored only one point. I'd picked up two fouls. Kellie Jolly kept us in the game with some great shooting and terrific ball handling.

We came out in the second half and scored the first seven points. After a dogfight struggle, we cut the Duke lead to two. We were rebounding better the second half, but our shots still weren't falling as they normally did. On one play, Semeka shot from outside, and missed. But Chamique grabbed the long rebound and shot a 15-foot jumper. And missed. But I grabbed that rebound right under the basket and put the ball back up. And missed. Only I grabbed my own rebound, and put the ball right back up. And I missed. Four shots. No points. It was that kind of game.

Chamique was our top scorer and team leader and naturally she tried to take the responsibility on herself. There's something to be said for shooting yourself into a rhythm, but there's also a point where you have to understand you might just not have it that night and you need to pass it off to others. In any case, Chamique kept trying to shoot herself into a rhythm. And her shots just didn't connect.

With about eight minutes to go, Kellie Jolly slid in for a layup and cut the Duke lead to one.

But Duke had weathered our comeback storm. Their big center, Van Gorp, had been pulled out of the game with four fouls but came back in with a few minutes to go. They scored a couple of threes from outside.

Our deficit climbed to seven points.

We were desperate. With about a half minute left, I launched a three and it fell in. But Duke scored again, and then Chamique fouled out. After winning three championships at Tennessee, she would go home empty her senior year.

Later, people would look back at the game, and there'd be so much analysis of what went wrong. But ultimately we knew we'd just blown it. Hard as we played, we didn't play smart. And all the expectations, hopes, and dreams we had for ourselves and for a four-peat were left in pieces on the basketball court in Greensboro.

The loss marked the end of Pat Summitt's run of consecutive NCAA championship titles. It marked the last games at Tennessee for Chamique and Kellie.

And it would mark the beginning of a new role for me in my final two years at Tennessee.

We were down to two Meeks, and it wasn't the same.

Chamique had always been the go-to person. She was the one we'd pass the ball to when we personally were in trouble on the court. When the other team's defense was solid, the ball would swing around from one of us to another, each of us looking for our shot and not finding it, until finally the ball would be passed over to Chamique. As the go-to girl, she had to make her shot even if her shot wasn't there. She knew that when the ball came to her, she had to deliver. When the pressure was on, she had to face it, stand up to it, and perform.

Chamique's graduation and entry into the WNBA meant the Fab 4 and others on the team had to step up. It meant *I* had to step up.

Pat talked with me before the season. She told me, "Now that Chamique is gone, they're gonna be gunning for you. You're the All-American. You're gonna get banged up, they'll be double- and triple-teaming you. You have to rise above it."

It meant that I was the new go-to girl.

I learned a lot about "rising above" in my last two years of college ball. I'm not sure at first I was comfortable being the go-to for the Lady Vols. I didn't doubt the talent God had given me, but to take the responsibility *for the team* was another thing.

I've since come to think that this is kind of like taking a leap of faith.

I think everyone needs to be a go-to person at some point. We all need to step up, stand for something, be the go-to for someone, and take responsibility. But some people have never taken control of their own lives to be that go-to person. Many don't take ownership of that.

In basketball, for me, it was a leap of faith. I had to dare myself to step up and be the go-to person. It's scary sometimes. It's challenging. But a leap of faith is when we jump and God says, "I've got you." A leap of faith is God saying, "I created you to be who you are. You can do this. Don't shrink from this opportunity in your life."

At the same time, a go-to person needs to understand that while there are times she has to be the one to face the pressure, step up to the challenge, and take the shot, there are also many times she has to be a team player. Success on the court depends on knowing which is which—knowing when you are the go-to and have to take the shot or when the team is made better by you passing the ball and being a team player.

I think success in life is the same thing. Knowing when to "take the shot." And knowing when to be a team player. At home. With family. With friends. At church. At play. At work.

My life was changing. And my focus too.

As I was walking around one of our dorm halls one day, I saw a young man crutching his way into the dorm. I don't know what it was that made me reach out to him to ask if he needed any help. But we started talking and formed an instant bond. He was in a rush but invited me to come to a "meeting" with him. I don't normally go with strangers, but for whatever reason, I matched his stride and joined him.

"Hi, my name is Tamika Catchings and I'm a junior here playing on the basketball team. Jeremy," I said as I looked over at him, "is how I got here."

That was my first of many meetings with FCA—Fellowship of Christian Athletes. FCA conducted meetings for athletes on campus called "huddles," where there would be Bible study, devotional time, speakers, and discussion. The best part to me was that it was *all* the other athletes—male and female, from all the different sports. I loved it!

I had a new focus for my life. Jesus was at the center, and I was more open with others about my faith. I'm not saying that I was sharing my testimony with everyone—I've never been one to be extremely vocal about much of anything, and besides, I knew how some Christians come across to others, and I didn't want to be too pushy like that. But I had found the most important thing in life, Jesus, and I didn't care if others knew.

It was an opportunity for me to learn more about God, Jesus, and the Bible. I think growing up we kind of have a child's view of God, based on Bible stories in Sunday school, and that's fine. But when we become adults, we need to step up to another level of knowledge and faith. That's what was happening to me, and that's what FCA helped me do.

Sometimes Ace, Semeka, and Tree attended FCA with me. For Ace, growing up, she really never read the Bible. Scripture was read in the Catholic church she attended, but the people didn't read it on their own. She was finding a depth of Bible understanding she never had before.

The Bible talks about spiritual "milk" and "solid food," how there's a simple faith that is about drinking "milk," yet how important it is to partake of the "solid food" of Scripture and grow a more adult faith.

That's what was happening to us.

One development was of real interest to all of us on the team.

Professional women's basketball became a reality in 1997. Commissioned by the NBA (National Basketball Association) in 1996, the WNBA was born. It launched with a marketing campaign—"We Got Next." Three stars were the faces of the new WNBA—Sheryl Swoopes, Rebecca Lobo, and Lisa Leslie.

By the fall of 1998, the WNBA was finishing their second year, with the Houston Comets winning back-to-back championship series.

The significance of the WNBA was not lost on us. At the time I'd accepted the letter of recruitment to play for Pat Summitt at Tennessee, there was nowhere for women to play professional basketball after college, except for international leagues and the Olympics once every four years. Now there was another path. New opportunity. Life after college. A career in basketball.

"One day I'll be in the NBA" was now a possibility in a way I hadn't imagined. My goal had changed to "One day I'll be in the WNBA."

The record we achieved my junior year was by many standards pretty great. We went 31–3.

Unfortunately, we lost our first regular-season game that year to Louisiana Tech, which, following our NCAA tournament loss the year before, prompted the media to wonder if we'd lost our winning ways. But we survived that, and won eleven straight before falling to archrival UConn. We also lost, badly, to Georgia, before going on another run of twenty straight wins and taking the number one seed going into the NCAA tournament.

Of course, the real problem was that the standards Pat set for us and that we had achieved in 1998 were so high that nothing short of perfection was perceived by the sports world and by the media as being significant enough.

And the competition level was getting higher.

Whether it was the success of the Lady Vols through the decade, the emergence of Geno Auriemma's UConn as a national force, or the growth of the newborn WNBA, women's basketball was growing fans, followers, and future basketball players. Now that there was a future career in the sport, the talent level had taken a leap forward.

We were facing better competition across the board. But we also picked up some top talent ourselves.

Pat had recruited Kara Lawson, a high school All-American guard from Springfield, Virginia. She was the top-ranked prospect that year, and she defied her father's wishes in choosing Tennessee over Stanford. Kara would come into the team her freshman year and immediately become the floor general and one of our top scorers. She had poise and lots of talent.

Tree had transferred out of Tennessee, going into her junior year at the University of South Carolina, where she had a great final two years. But in her absence, Michelle Snow stepped up and became our strong presence in the middle.

Without Tree, our Fab 4 suddenly became a Fab 3, not quite the same. But Ace, Semeka, and I were starters that year, with Kara and Michelle rounding out our starting five. As a team, we were a strong shooting team averaging nearly eighty points a game.

The NCAA tournament took us from Knoxville to Memphis and landed us in Philadelphia for the championship game against our archrival, UConn. We won every game by double digits, and we felt good about our chances in the final.

Ace hurt her ankle that morning in shoot-around, and besides the obvious loss of her leadership on the court, we hoped it wasn't an omen of the game to come. Mique was at the game, this time watching, fresh off her first season with the WNBA Washington Mystics and being named WNBA Rookie of the Year. Perhaps that would give us the motivational edge we needed.

UConn came out playing relentless defense. Smothering. Scrappy. Maybe they took a page out of Duke's playbook the year before. Led by guard Sue Bird, they relentlessly pushed the ball up the court after forcing us to turn over the ball, and often scoring on their end. We had twelve turnovers in the first half, and I'd bet UConn converted most of them into points.

I had defenders draped all over me. I fought and scraped to get free, and rarely did. It made me so frustrated. After the first sixteen minutes of play I hadn't scored yet. Semeka was also having a bad night, with just two points.

We went nearly eight minutes without scoring a basket. I remembered what Pat had told me at the beginning of the year. How I needed to rise above. I kept playing through, playing hard, trying to find a zone.

And then, I had a brief flurry of success toward the end of the first half. I scored, finally, and after a stop at the other end, Kara fed me a bounce pass and I drained a three.

Even so, we went into the locker room at halftime down by fifteen. Not that it was a deficit we couldn't overcome, but nothing we'd done in the first half gave anyone confidence we could turn things around.

I won't say much about the second half. It was all UConn. They played a great game, and we just didn't put it together. With five minutes to go in the game we were down by twenty-five. It was not only frustrating; it was embarrassing. And no matter how frantically we played in the final minutes, we would lose the championship by nineteen points.

I was asked after the game how I felt. I suppose it's the obvious question, but really? I felt bad. Really bad.

Have I mentioned how much I hate to lose?

Dealing with losing is a part of life. I say that while at the same time I admit that sometimes I am a terrible loser. The one thing I've learned is that it's really important not to get too down on yourself. It's easy to swallow a loss and let it spoil inside you. You can start to doubt yourself, question your ability, and become tentative about what you're made to do. You have to move on.

I think it's best to focus instead on what you have achieved, relish those moments of excellence when you know you did your best, and embrace the underlying talent that is your joy. Sometimes that's hard to do, especially after a tough loss. But you just have to rise above. Fighting off the negative energy following a loss is sometimes as important as the battle during the game. Remember, the important thing is not how many times you get knocked down but how many times you choose to get back up.

That year I was honored by being selected as the Naismith College Player of the Year. It's a prestigious honor, a selection of the top coaches, sports media, and fans across the country. The award was a reflection of how others recognized the level of play I had reached and meant that I had established myself at the top of the college game.

It was also special to me because the winner both of the previous years was Chamique Holdsclaw.

I had become the go-to girl.

We entered the new millennium with high hopes for reclaiming the NCAA championship title. Semeka, Ace, and I were seniors, veterans of the Pat Summitt era. Kara Lawson was a sophomore, along with an emerging forward from Alabama named Gwen Jackson. Michelle Snow continued as our force in the middle, along with freshman center Ashley Robinson.

We beat our first five opponents by an average of thirty-three points. Everything was clicking. All five of us starters were each scoring in double digits.

One of those early games was against Illinois. But my sister Tauja had graduated that spring after a strong college career with the Illini, and was drafted by the WNBA Phoenix Mercury. (That one game back in 1998 when Tennessee and Illinois faced off would be the only time Tauja and I competed head-to-head on a college court.)

There was talk about who would be the top picks in the WNBA draft the next year. Some top players were mentioned in the discussions—Jackie Stiles, Katie Douglas, Australia's Lauren Jackson, and Kelly Miller, among others, including me. In fact, some talked about me going number one. I really didn't think about it much, but I was confident enough that I could be one of the top picks in the draft that next April.

But my focus was on playing games now, and winning for Tennessee. Which we did. In fact, we'd win our first eleven games of the year—before coming to a screeching halt in none other than Storrs, Connecticut, at the hands of our archnemesis, UConn.

After the loss to Connecticut, we'd win our next four games before facing Mississippi State on January 15.

We were playing at home on a cloudy, dreary day in Knoxville. We started the game slowly, and were actually behind the entire first half. Six assists in the first half was the sorry stat stating the obvious—we weren't passing the ball enough, not working together as a team.

But we came out the second half on fire. Went on something like a 9–0 run and finally tied it some four minutes in. With a little under seven minutes left in the game, we were up by eight. A lead, but not our normal blowout. It was that kind of game, like playing in molasses. Eight points was about as big a lead as we'd had all night. But we knew it wasn't safe.

On defense I was able to slide into position under the basket just in time to take a charge from the Bulldogs' guard LaToya Thomas. We got two out of that, extending our lead to ten. But Mississippi State's Cynthia Hall scored a big three-pointer to cut it to just seven.

We needed to answer.

As the ball came out of the net, it was quickly inbounded to me, and I raced up the floor, dribbling on the right side. I had position, the only thing between me and the basket was LaToya, and then I would have a clear path to the basket. I remember going at her with an in and out right past half-court and getting by her. As I got to the basket I came in and jump-stopped.

I planted my feet. And then, going up, I felt something in my knee.

My strength rushed out of my leg. I lost upward momentum, and the ball never had a chance. I came down in a heap, writhing in pain. Later, spectators and announcers would speculate that I hurt myself as I hit the floor. Not so. I was hurt on the way up. I felt the pain.

After some minutes, the pain had subsided. Had I thought about it, I'd have realized it only subsided because I wasn't moving my knee. Keeping it in one place, it felt relatively okay. I begged everyone to tape me up and let me keep playing. But no one would listen. They knew better. What it looked like, what they feared, and what turned out to be true was that I had torn my ACL.

I was carted off the court. It was a season-ending injury, not to mention having serious implications regarding my future status in the WNBA.

It was an experience that would change my perspective and my life, although it certainly wouldn't be the last time I'd have my shot blocked by God.

Part 4

VOICES

They're everywhere . . .
The voices, the murmurs they continue on
I don't quite understand, but they're there. I hear them.
In my head, from my fam . . . Go left. Go right. Shoot. Drive.
Be the shooter. Don't pass up shots.
Defend. Shoot. Go, go, go . . .

12

FEVER

You're blessed when you're at the end of your rope. With less of you there is more of God and his rule.

Matthew 5:3, Message

We take so much for granted in life, assuming that we will be able to do this and that, and that tomorrow we will be able to do more of what we did today, and that we'll be able to continue our life on the course it's on.

I felt so many things in the aftermath of my injury. Anger, confusion, worry. Why did it have to happen *now*? I had hoped to finish out my last year at Tennessee in a flourish, maybe lead the team to another national championship. And I had dreamed of being picked up by a top team in the WNBA draft. Now those hopes and dreams lay in pieces underneath the basket alongside my shattered ACL.

The Tennessee Lady Vols would have to finish the season without me. And no WNBA team would want to draft a player with a shattered ACL.

Tearing my ACL was devastating in so many ways.

It's a common injury in sports, especially in basketball, especially among women, as it turns out—an injury to the part of the knee that stabilizes it. I might have assumed it would happen sometime in my basketball career, but I never imagined it would happen like that or at that time. ACLs require a long recovery time and tons of rehab. I could handle the recovery work, but what about my future career in basketball?

A verse in the Bible says something like, "You don't know what your life will be like tomorrow. Your life is like the morning fog—it's here a little while, then it's gone."[1] In the aftermath of my injury, I was in that Knoxville fog, frustrated and disappointed. And I think maybe I caught a glimpse of how fleeting and fragile life actually is.

That became God time for me. I had to turn to God for understanding about what had happened. I sought him, prayed, and did the only other thing I could do: wait. Times like these give the phrase "Wait upon the Lord" new meaning.

I don't know that God causes things like my injury, but I sure know he uses them. When I wasn't completely consumed with basketball, suddenly my heart turned to him once again. And I felt called to give him my life, completely.

And it was then that I felt a change. My anger and confusion fell away. I literally felt, suddenly, that I was washed in peace.

The Lady Vols played well without me. I had been their leading scorer, and it wasn't easy to replace my average fifteen

points per game. But the team stepped up. We won the remainder of our games in the regular season, faltering only
in the SEC tournament game against Vandy, a loss of just
three points.

Entering the NCAA tournament that year, the Lady Vols
retained our number one seed in the Mideast Regionals and
quickly dispatched sixteenth seed Austin Peay and ninth seed
St Mary's. But in the regional, we faced Xavier and were
trounced by fifteen points.

Another championship had eluded Pat Summitt for another year.

And I would not play another game for the Tennessee
Lady Vols.

The disappointment of Tennessee blended into my fears
about the WNBA draft. When the injury occurred and I
realized it would sideline me for nearly a year, I was crest-
fallen. I knew it would severely lessen my chances of being
drafted.

The summer before, I had done an internship with the
WNBA Phoenix Mercury, the team that had drafted my sister,
Tauja. As it happened, Tauja was cut from the team right
before that season (later to be picked up and then cut by the
Miami Sol), but I was committed to the internship in Phoenix
and did it anyway. It contributed to my degree.

In fact, at Tennessee I finished my undergraduate degree
early, and for the second half of my senior year I started
working on a master's in sports management. The internship in Phoenix gave me a firsthand look at the management
of a pro team. That summer I also learned a lot about the

commercial realities of a pro team and what they looked for in drafting.

The WNBA was brand new, trying to establish itself, draw fans, bulk up attendance. A lot of WNBA teams were marginal financially, and needed all the paying fans they could draw. They needed collegiate stars to draw interest in their teams. Most of all, they needed collegiate stars *who would actually play*, not sit out a year to get a knee mended.

I compared it to going to the store—if you walk in to buy something, you want it to be new, not used and broken. WNBA teams likewise drafted for the new, not the used and broken, player. So I knew my stock in the draft had taken a hit, and I didn't know where I'd place in the draft order, if I placed at all. Deep inside, I feared no one would want me.

It was all so . . . frustrating.

There's a verse in *The Message* version of the Bible where Jesus said, "You're blessed when you're at the end of your rope. With less of you there is more of God" (Matt. 5:3). I wasn't so sure yet about the blessing part, but my injury made sure there was "less of me" on the court with Tennessee, and perhaps this would prove to be true in the WNBA as well.

It's always been a struggle between God and me. Some have said I'm kind of stubborn. (Actually, some say I'm a *lot* stubborn.) I want to control my life, what I do, where I'm going. It's hard for me to let go of that. So when I wrestle with God, I don't give in easily.

But then he is . . . well, God.

There wasn't much I could do. But there was a lot God could do. And he did.

The WNBA draft was held in Secaucus, New Jersey. Despite my injury and fading draft hopes, I had an invite to attend. I went, even though I had mixed feelings. I wanted to be part of the excitement and the festivities. But I wasn't sure I would really be a part of anything, given my draft chances. And it was possible that where I landed in the draft could really disappoint my lifetime of dreams.

My parents were there to cheer me on. It was in a large TV studio housed by NBA Entertainment, and dozens of college players were there, along with friends and family. We each awaited our fate—a lottery ticket that in some cases would determine where someone would live and play and settle down for years to come.

The first pick was owned by the Seattle Storm, and it was no surprise they selected the Australian basketball star Lauren Jackson. (A round later Seattle would select Semeka Randall as their number two pick.)

I was interested, of course, in the fortunes of those I had played with and against. But I also felt I was in for a long night. Waiting, and perhaps not being selected at all. Waiting for disappointment.

Up second, the Charlotte Sting picked guard Kelly Miller from Georgia.

Then the Indiana Fever were on the clock. And the announcement came quickly: "The Indiana Fever choose, as their first selection . . . Tamika Catchings from the University of Tennessee."

I couldn't believe it. After all my concerns and worries about being picked at all, I was picked *third*?

I had two immediate reactions. One was a shout for joy. The other was panic. I knew that in moments I'd be in front of a camera and a microphone with a reporter asking me to talk about how I felt to be going to Indiana. And *what did I know about Indiana*? I thought of farmland and cows and corn. What else? What city did the Fever play in? Oh, right. Indianapolis. Wasn't that where Purdue played? No. Not quite. University of Indiana? I think so. Oh, my!

I don't even remember what I said to the media. I guess it was okay. I would learn later how great a place Indianapolis, Indiana, was. In those moments, though, the point was that the Fever *wanted* me—despite the fact that I wouldn't be playing for them for a whole year. Quite a risk on their part.

And maybe that's partly why I've been so loyal to Indiana since. They believed in me. And I've given back to them. I've been with the Fever my whole pro career.

So long, in fact, that they now consider me an honorary Hoosier!

In retrospect, the frantic pace of those days and weeks is hard to imagine now:

- My last college game was January 15.
- My surgery was the day after Martin Luther King Jr. Day.
- The WNBA draft was just a few weeks later, on April 20.
- The Fever would start training camp a couple of weeks after that.
- The WNBA season would start May 31, though I would be watching, not playing.

Of course, there was this other little thing called *moving*. I would need to move out of my apartment, say good-bye to

Knoxville, and move to Somewhere, Indiana. And so, two weeks after the draft, I moved to an apartment in Indianapolis. Oh yes, and there was also this little thing called *graduation*. I would definitely be there to participate in the commencement ceremonies.

That was such a bittersweet experience. I guess all graduations are. You're leaving a place that became so much to you. A place that contained the legend Pat Summitt, who taught you so much more than basketball. A place where you grew up from being a girl to being a woman.

Three of us Fab 4, who had entered UT together four years earlier, were graduating not only from Tennessee but into the WNBA, Semeka going to Seattle and Ace going to Houston. Our futures lay before us, and our college experience stretched out behind us. But our friendship would continue. Both Semeka and Ace continue to be good friends to me to this day. It was a sad time but a happy time. We cried some tears. And we laughed about the things we'd done together.

And I think there's a special bond for those who have played at the top level of competition, who have endured pressure together, and who have reached the height of competitive play. We had gone through a lot together.

We'd be moving on. But to an even higher-level game. We would all meet again.

This time we'd play *against* each other.

One of four teams inaugurated in the 2000 season, the Fever was just getting established. The year before it had its start with players picked from an expansion draft. In an expansion draft the existing teams can protect five current top players. The remaining players go into the draft and are selected by the new franchises.

The Indiana Fever had the first pick that year before and wound up with some good players, but it's inevitable that the new teams would start slow and take some years to develop and draft top talent. In year one, its record was 9–23.

I was the first regular draft pick of the Indiana Fever. And I wouldn't be on the court for another year.

The Fever would struggle again in year two, finishing just one game better than it had its first year. I watched from the bench, itching to play. My recovery from my torn ACL was progressing normally, but "normal" for an impatient me was too slow.

In early July, I hit a benchmark and was cleared to run straight lanes. No cutting, no pounding, no sprinting, just a nice casual gait forward. I was too excited! Shortly after that, I joined the team on my first road trip to Houston, Texas, where we would be taking on the Comets the next day. We landed and headed straight to the gym for practice. This would be my first time as a player in another team's facility.

I was soaking up every moment. I changed clothes and waited for the rest of the team to get going so we could get on the court. I was mid-gait when I felt something tug in my knee. I tried to walk, but it hurt. It was a sharp pain in my knee and down my leg. Inside I was having a panic attack, outside I was looking around for our trainer—somewhat cool and somewhat frantically (if that's possible). When I finally located our trainer and told her the pain I was feeling, she checked my knee and the next thing I knew, I was on a plane headed back to Indianapolis. I was devastated. I didn't even get a chance to stay and watch our game against the Comets.

The doctor checked my knee and I found I had torn my meniscus. Another surgery required. More time before I would step back on the court. A complete letdown. But after being so close to the game in Houston, I was even more determined to get back. Another test from God.

My first chance at playing again would be early in 2002, in the off-season. I learned about another women's professional league, the National Women's Basketball League (NWBL) that was starting up and got a chance to head back to my hometown of Chicago and play with the Chicago Blaze. I was a little nervous as this would be my first competitive action since I tore my ACL, although I had fully recovered by now and had worked out and rehabbed hard.

Some people are surprised at the number of basketball leagues and competitions that exist in basketball outside of the NCAA and WNBA. But many different leagues in the United States and overseas are options for basketball players in the off-season. It's possible for a woman basketball player to play on different teams in different leagues in different competitions nearly year-round.

In March I traveled to Houston to try out for the United States Women's National Basketball Team. This team would represent the United States at the FIBA World Championships in China. If I made this team, and we won, I would get a shot at making the team two years later in the Olympics.

I didn't know this when I tried out, but I heard later that the coach of the U.S. team, Van Chancellor, also coach of the WNBA Houston Comets, was reluctant to invite me to play. It was because he didn't want to be responsible if my rehab wasn't complete and I got hurt again. He doubted I would, or even should, make the team.

It felt good to be invited to play with some of the top players—including Sheryl Swoopes, Dawn Staley, and Lisa Leslie. The competition was high.

It was said that as soon as Van Chancellor asked, "Why is Catchings here?" in his southern drawl, there was a loud screech. As everyone turned their heads, they could see I had slid and saved the ball—the hustle play I'm known for. And then he said, "Oh, yes, she can play." He said later he regretted doubting my fitness and ability to play at that level and kicked himself for nearly keeping me off the squad.

I made the team. And I thought about how much would have to happen in the next few months—my first year of pro basketball with the Indiana Fever and then at the break being ready to compete in the World Championships.

It had been a little more than a year since I tore my ACL. I thought about how much had happened in that year. I thought about how much God can do with us during the downtimes of our lives.

13

BUILDING

A lot of players are talented—everybody can shoot,
everybody can rebound—but it comes down to
how bad do you want it? There's just a relentlessness to Tamika's game that really blows you away.

Nell Fortner, head coach,
Indiana Fever, 1999–2003

There's a certain amount of pressure (a) being selected as a
number one draft pick for a pro team, (b) missing your first
year due to an injury, and (c) being looked at in the third year
of a new franchise as the savior of the franchise.

I felt that pressure, but I was also eager to get back on the
court and play. My experience at the USA World Championship tryouts gave me confidence in my knee, and I was ready
for my first season in the pros.

Nell Fortner was the Fever coach. In 1999, when the Fever was born as a franchise, she was named head coach and general manager. However, she was serving then as head coach for the 2000 USA team—the team headed for the Olympics—so she didn't coach during the Fever's first year. She was at the helm of the Fever my first year—the year I sat out. Now I was playing under her, not just watching her coach.

Nell was a highly motivational coach. She was always a positive person, always ready with an inspirational quote. She would find ways to encourage and nudge you forward.

One of my goals for the year was to get into the playoffs. You always want to win the championship, but realistically, there were going to be some challenges. The year before the Fever had gone 10–22, and we had a lot of work to do.

It felt good to play again. My knee was fine, and I enjoyed playing at a higher level of competition. The WNBA drafted only sixty-four players each year; the league represents the top 1 percent of college women's basketball players. So I was indeed playing against the best.

In the midst of my first season, we had to take a hiatus for the World Championships. The tournament was held in China, and along with being the defensive specialist, I wound up the second-leading rebounder and the third-leading scorer. With the great talent we had, we swept everyone off the court and won the World Championships.

When the Fever resumed league play, the good news was that we had the best season in franchise history, finishing 16–16 for the regular season. And yes, we made it into the playoffs—barely. We tied with the Orlando Miracle for the final playoff spot and faced them in a tiebreaker game. We won and made a playoff berth for the first time in Fever history—only to fall in the first round against number one seed New York Liberty, who made it to the finals that year.

One honor that meant a lot to me in 2002 was winning WNBA Rookie of the Year. Considering the level of talent recruited in 2001 and 2002, and given that I had to overcome the ACL and meniscus injuries, it was an accomplishment I would be very proud of.

Someone said back then that I "willed" the team into the playoffs. I'm not sure about that. I worked hard, played hard, competed hard. That's what I know how to do.

At that time in my life and my career I didn't think of myself as a leader. I knew I had the talent to move the team forward and I worked hard to achieve what I wanted to go after. But I never really thought much back then about what I needed to do to motivate others. If I led anyone, it was by example, by how I practiced and played, not by words I said or challenges I issued or calling anyone to task for not working hard enough.

So I don't know what to say about "willing the team" into the playoffs. I suppose I shouldered my share of the effort, and maybe more than my share. I simply wanted it. You play to win.

Later I would learn a lesson in leadership—up front, outspoken, lead-the-team leadership—but it wouldn't be for another couple of years.

For now I was just a rookie who played hard and wanted to win.

Indy is a small enough, but big enough, city that I got plenty of attention as a professional player, but not so much media pressure as would be the case if I played in New York or LA. My dad would say it was a blessing I didn't get drafted by the Liberty or the Sparks, the teams in the big cities where the lights of the media are intense and searing. Even so, being Rookie of the Year and the Fever getting into the playoffs for the first time generated a lot of excitement and I could feel the cameras on me.

I was a long way away from my childhood years of wearing huge hearing aids and being made fun of. Yet I still was not comfortable with all the attention.

But Tauja was there—always on my side.

She had chosen to come back from playing abroad in Valenciennes, France, when I tore my ACL. She moved with me from Tennessee to Indianapolis to help in the pursuit of my professional basketball dreams. We shared an apartment in Indianapolis, and she was a rock for me in those early years. Most of all, it was the beginning of a recovery of our deep relationship as sisters after years separated by divorce and playing on competing teams in the NCAA.

During my ACL recovery, I had time on my hands. I talked to our Fever community relations director about opportunities to be engaged in the Indianapolis community, and that's where I found myself in conversation with one of the city's park managers after a team appearance with the youth. He tossed out the idea of me starting a basketball camp for inner-city kids. I went home to Tauja, excited about the possibility. In fact, that was something we had talked about years earlier when we were kids. I had dreamed that one day I would be able to host my own "Tamika Catchings Basketball Camp." Now the idea of a youth basketball camp didn't seem so crazy. It seemed completely possible.

We put together a plan and spread the word about a five-day camp in December. Tauja was amazing in figuring out how to do it. As I've always said, I'm good at basketball; Tauja's good at everything. She just has a great deal of know-how about how to organize and make things happen.

The camp was amazing, though exhausting—every day with kids, all day, for five days (how do teachers do it?)—but afterward we got so much positive feedback from parents. So much positive feedback that the parents asked for more programming for their kids.

Tauja and I put our heads together, and the next year we added a "fitness" clinic. Indiana ranks high in incidence of childhood obesity, and we wanted to address that. At the same time we wanted to help kids learn about exercise and fitness, we knew we were working in some challenged areas of the city, working with families who often didn't have money for basketball camps and such. So we made the fitness clinic "free." All the family had to do to earn admission for their kids was to donate ten cans of food.

And we would make, as part of the clinic activities, an exercise of bringing those cans to a local food bank. These kids were so often themselves in need and looking for a handout. Now just to see the look on those kids' faces as they put those cans on the scale at the food bank was priceless.

To see them experience the joy of giving back made me start to feel that this is what we were really made to do. Purpose.

That winter was cold and blustery, as Indiana winters always are, and it blew in the winds of change for the Fever in 2003.

Nell Fortner resigned as coach. Kelly Krauskopf, who had been director of business operations for the Fever from the beginning, hired Brian Winters as our new head coach. Brian had played with my dad when he was with the Milwaukee Bucks. He was a quiet, self-contained type of coach, given to the x's and o's of the game. He was so calm and even-keeled that when he did get upset, you knew it.

The team added new players as well, including Natalie Williams and Kelly Miller. Natalie was a forward who'd made her mark as a franchise player with the Utah Starzz and was a former Olympian too. Kelly was a super quick guard who was originally drafted the same year I was, right ahead of me at number two to the Charlotte Sting.

With changes in the front office, the head coach, and on the court, there was a lot of excitement about the new Fever. And we started to draw some new fans. Our opening day game on May 29 that year was a sellout—the first in franchise history. Unfortunately we lost that game against the Charlotte Sting.

Our second game that year was broadcast on national television, against the Washington Mystics, and we won by eleven points.

I think we were better that year, better in terms of the level of our play, but our record didn't show it. We finished 16–18 and missed the playoffs.

While it was disappointing, over the years I've learned that through ball and life, sometimes we *are* better than before, but maybe the results don't show it. It's like when you work on some part of your game—say, defense. When I went to Tennessee and had that run-in with Pat about my technique, she was teaching me a new way to play defense. As I tried to play her way, it felt awkward at first, unnatural. I think it was better technique, but it didn't feel that way, and it took a while before it had its effect on the court. Fortunately I stuck with it—Pat made sure of that—and the results eventually came around.

In life we might strive to get better at something—at work, or in competition, or in marriage—and we make changes in ourselves. But we often don't see the results of those changes immediately. It requires us to be patient. To follow through. To be consistent.

The Bible says "The fruit of the Spirit is love, joy, peace, forbearance, kindness, goodness, faithfulness, gentleness and self-control" (Gal. 5:22–23 NIV).

With the Indiana Fever in 2003, I needed to realize that though we were better, the fruit of our efforts would take some more time to develop. I needed to be patient.

There was only one problem.

I don't do "patience" very well.

The year 2004 was another mixed-results season for the Fever, and one that would again test my patience. It would also be my first time at the Olympics, an amazing experience. In August, the WNBA took a hiatus and players representing their respective countries flew to Athens, Greece, for the Olympic Games. I was so excited to be joining my fellow USA teammates.

Athens, as the birthplace of the Olympics, was an especially meaningful location, and it was simply an overwhelming kaleidoscope of color and pageantry. The opening ceremony, held in the Olympic Stadium, was incredible.

The massive structure, a lacework of metal cables and steel at the sides and overhang, featured a huge white oval in the center. As the countries' teams marched in, we paraded around the track and spiraled into the center oval. The flags and costumes of each country's athletes were colorful and fascinating, and the sound and music simply created a feeling of awe.

Dawn Staley, from the women's basketball team, was selected to lead *all* the U.S. athletes into the stadium. It was an incredible experience that impressed on me the variety of people, "all God's children," in the world. And I was so proud and honored to be there representing the USA.

Tauja and my mom were there with me as well, which made the experience all the richer. The U.S. men's and women's basketball teams had chosen not to stay in the Olympic Village housing, as that was deemed to be a distraction and not conducive to prep for our competitions. Instead we stayed on a chartered ship, the Queen Mary II, docked in the harbor of the Aegean Sea, off the coast of Athens.

As we prepared to keep the gold medal streak alive (the team had won gold in 1996 and 2000), we knew the international competition had upped its game. We might be challenged, but we would be prepared. While I would remember this Olympics as my first, I would also remember it for my first true individual challenge as a player and a huge lesson in leadership.

The Olympic team was composed of a wealth of talent. Players like Dawn Staley, Lisa Leslie, Sheryl Swoopes, Sue Bird, Diana Taurasi, me, and so many others—we all had to put aside our egos to play together and focus on the ultimate goal: the gold.

I never considered myself a born leader but more of a "quiet leader by example." What I've seen is that sometimes your talent and your success push you into a more visible and more aggressive leadership role. I'd been feeling that the Fever needed that kind of leadership from me. I just didn't know how to give it. I was content to lead behind the scenes, a leader who *shows* you rather than tells you. But sometimes we're called to be more outspoken and to lead more directly. And that's not always comfortable.

I see that when it comes to our faith too. We hope to live a life that's a good example, one that reflects Jesus to others. There is certainly a place for the kind of faith that doesn't hit people over the head with your beliefs. Yet sometimes we're called to be more outspoken and to "lead others" with a more open statement of what Jesus means to us. All this is fine and good, but sometimes we're just not comfortable with it, and often we don't quite know how to go about doing it. Sometimes we need to see it demonstrated to see how it works.

At the Olympic Games I watched Dawn Staley in action. And learned what it takes to be a true leader.

She had the confidence to take the lead with a group of basketball stars who were themselves leaders on their individual WNBA teams. That year at the Olympics, I watched and listened as she pulled together all these different personalities. She'd tell each of us how we needed to play a role on this team—perhaps a role that we weren't used to back home. Dawn would talk personally to each one of us and say, "Here's what I need you to do."

I remember Dawn pulling me to the side and telling me, "Catch, you just have to play your game. I know it's easier said than done, but we need you. If you do your part, then we're gonna win." I believed in Dawn, my teammates, and the opportunity ahead of us. I would not let them down.

A head coach can do only so much. He or she can train you, motivate you, challenge you. But every coach needs a leader on the court. Dawn was that leader for our 2004 Olympics team.

Our toughest game was against Russia in the semifinals, but we won by four points. And we beat Australia in the gold medal round by eleven.

I would have a gold medal around my neck, but as amazing as that was, I'd come back with something far more valuable. I would not be the leading scorer or the leading rebounder or the leader in steals at the Olympics that year.

But I'd be returning home a leader in a whole different way than I had been before.

The biggest thing for me in 2004 wasn't on the court.

The community initiatives Tauja and I had started were evolving into something bigger. We now had basketball camps, fitness clinics, and mentoring programs, and we continued to add more programs. In fall 2004, we received 501(c) (3) status for our nonprofit, the Catch the Stars Foundation. From the beginning, Tauja and I were the dynamic duo, but she was the driving force, helping to do nearly everything needed to keep this dream alive.

When I was a kid, I had to overcome a lot of obstacles like low self-esteem and bullying and struggled to find my place, but I was able to use all those obstacles to fuel my success later on in life. While most kids didn't have to deal with a hearing loss, many needed to overcome other barriers, most of all, a lack of opportunity. My goal was to inspire and uplift youth. My goal was to help Indy's youth define purpose and achieve their potential by providing goal-setting programs that promote literacy, fitness, and mentoring; to help them to set goals and "catch their dreams one star at a time."

14

RELATIONSHIPS

The face of the Fever is Tamika Catchings! She is my kind of player, relentless in her pursuit of excellence. Determined and dedicated, she defends and rebounds with a passion unequaled. And, off the court, she gives back to her fans and her community more than any athlete I have ever coached.

Lin Dunn, Indiana Fever head
coach, 2008–2014

The five players on the court have to have the same dream. Not just that we all want to win (of course!), but a collective dream about *how we are to play together to win.* That requires the players to play their roles, to find their spots, to move not individually but in relationship to each other.

If football is rock music, and baseball is classical music, then basketball is jazz. Jazz is an ensemble of people improvising all at the same time, each doing her own thing, but together. That's what makes it hard. On the court, you need to do what you do best, but do it in rhythm with everyone else. In 2005, the Fever played some pretty good jazz. We wound up with a 21–13 record and made the playoffs for the second time. In the postseason, we swept the New York Liberty, which was our first playoff series win. But in the next series against the Connecticut Sun, we lost the first game in the final seconds as the Sun's star Katie Douglas sank a winning three.

A step forward, but frustrating.

Do you want to date me because I'm "Tamika" or "Tamika Catchings"?

Flying solo wasn't the same now as it might have been in high school or college. I was a celebrity and becoming a well-known star in the Indianapolis area. Guys would approach me and ask me out. I had to figure out why and what they were interested in. Whatever they actually called me, I could tell if they might be interested in the real "Tamika" or in the celebrity "Tamika Catchings."

Not that I ever made it easy to get to know me.

I know sports have always been my buffer against life, a bubble I lived inside where I could not be touched. From my early years in school, the court was where I could level my opposition, where my basketball achievements earned me respect. My bubble world of basketball was the safe house of my life.

I always had that bubble wall around me. I know I tend not to let that wall down. It's scary out there, and you don't want to get hurt, so you crawl into your bubble world and protect yourself. I know that's an issue for me. But it is what it is.

So it's been a long time since I've allowed someone I've dated to be a part of, like, my *life*. Not my public life—everyone has a piece of that. My private me. Tamika. My *life*. What some guys don't understand is that if I let them in, their lives change too. Here's the thing about the bubble—it's transparent and everyone can see what you do. So if you want to enter my life, my real life, you need to know everyone's watching. Everyone becomes a judge. Everyone has an opinion about me. You. You and me. And then I get protective and ready for battle.

Relationships take a lot of work.

In the off-season, the Fever made a number of changes. They acquired free agent Tamika Whitmore of the LA Sparks. Suddenly I wasn't the only Tamika on the team. Whitmore had been a star forward for the New York Liberty and the LA Sparks, a strong shooter, and promised to be a strong addition to the Fever.

Year after year, we were striving to reach the pinnacle of winning a championship. For the front office, the coaching staff, and me, there was this sense of building something, climbing a ladder to the top.

In 2006, we would duplicate our previous season record: 21–13. A good record overall, but not better, not a step up. With all the changes, it was tough not to improve at least a little. Frustrating.

And, to make matters worse, we crashed and burned in the playoffs. Facing our archrival Detroit (we'd placed second and third in the standings), we lost the first game of the best of three. In the second game Tamika Whitmore would set a WNBA scoring record—forty-one points—and yet we'd lose by a big margin.

That season would be the second year in a row that I'd be awarded the WNBA's "Defensive Player of the Year" award—an honor that had me recalling my first and only run-in with Pat Summitt some nine years earlier, as she tried to teach this defiant teenage girl how to play proper defense.

But the highlight of my 2006 had to be the All-Star game. While I've been fortunate to be selected for many All-Star teams during my career, this was special because it was held in New York's Madison Square Garden. Great sports figures had played there—Muhammed Ali, Joe Frazier, Patrick Ewing—not to mention a number of NHL and NBA All-Star teams. Now we were on that same court, playing professional basketball in front of thousands.

Katie Douglas was named MVP of the game. I was selected to the WNBA "All-Decade Team." It was a great honor to receive this recognition at halftime alongside Dawn Staley, Sheryl Swoopes, Lisa Leslie, and many other notable stars.

It felt good to be chosen.

In a way, your family doesn't choose you. You are born into them, and they have to deal with you. If you're lucky, like me, your mom and dad love you just because you're theirs, and maybe they're proud of you no matter what. But your brothers and sisters can invite you into their lives, or not.

They can live in ways that make you important to them, or not. They can choose you, or not.

In all my basketball career—my high school and then college successes, and now in my pro ball career—there's been one "fan" who's often been in the background, sometimes sitting at courtside with his kids, sometimes unable to be there physically but still there emotionally and spiritually, in his own special way.

My brother, Kenyon. He chose me then, and he has continued to choose me throughout my life. His support means the world to me.

I have always had the sense that for both Kenyon and Tauja, I got the basketball fame they might have had. Tauja was such a good basketball player, but she chose not to pursue it. She didn't have the passion for the game like Kenyon and I did. Plus, she excels in so many other things. She amazes me. Kenyon, though, would have been in the NBA if not for his Crohn's disease. It derailed his basketball career and changed his life.

Between junior and senior year in high school Kenyon was in and out of the hospital, looking for answers. Crohn's, a nasty inflammatory intestinal disease that cannot be cured but only controlled, changed his options. Yes, he got better, but his dreams of playing ball were shattered. Despite his struggle with Crohn's, he had always planned for his next phase in life. He knew basketball wasn't his only option. He studied hard, excelled academically, and won a scholarship to Northern Illinois University. He started his dream life with Motorola and since then has developed a distinguished career in the pharmaceutical industry, settling in St. Louis and growing a family.

Kenyon—quiet, gentle, yet so strong—lets me know frequently that he chooses me, by his phone calls every day, our conversations, and coming to Indianapolis just to hang out. I don't assume that basketball is the only important thing in the world. I know better than that. I don't assume that basketball is the highest goal or dream for Tauja or for Kenyon that they weren't able or did not want to realize. But I do have a sense that in a family whose destiny for so long revolved around an orange ball, I was the one who wound up with the basketball opportunity and the life in the sport. I was the youngest child in a basketball family, the little girl with big box hearing aids who would someday land among the stars.

Ultimately, the only thing that matters is to excel in the thing God wants you to do and made you to do. All three of us have and continue to do that in our own unique ways.

And so Kenyon is there for me, courtside with his boys, cheering me on, or back home, cheering me on. In his heart and soul, cheering me on. And more and more I'm aware he has the life of children and family that I can only hope to have myself someday.

Kenyon, I choose you too.

In 2007 the Fever, right out of the gate, had the strongest run of basketball in its young history. We won sixteen out of our first twenty games—the best start in the eastern conference.

One of our new players was Tammy Sutton-Brown. She had played for the Charlotte Sting, a franchise that just didn't thrive and folded after the 2006 season. When Tammy became available, the Fever picked her up.

Not only did Tammy become a standout center for the Fever, she also became one of my best friends. From the beginning, something with us just clicked. She shared my passion for hard work and my deep dislike of anything that smacked of mediocrity. She also had a heart for kids, eventually establishing her own basketball camp program and writing children's books. We seemed to look at life and basketball through the same set of glasses.

On July 20 that year, I injured my foot. It was a partial tear of my plantar fascia, which is the flat connective tissue on the bottom of the foot. In short, it was an injury to the arch of my foot, very painful, needing weeks to heal.

The Fever would go 5–9 the remainder of the regular season. Still, we got into the playoffs, encountering the Connecticut Sun in the first round, for a remarkable series of games. And I was able to recover well enough to play.

The first game was a classic—it went to three overtimes, a marathon back-and-forth game, exciting in every respect. The Sun ultimately bested us by about five points. But the Fever took the second game handily, winning by nearly twenty points.

It was game three that would prove what inner soul the Fever really had. At one point in the second quarter we were down by twenty-two points. No team had ever come back from that size of a deficit before. By statistical standards, we were doomed. Katie Douglas and some of the other Sun players sensed that, too, and started talking trash.

We didn't like that.

We stayed focused, playing hard, chipping away at the Sun's lead. Slowly we crept back into it, cutting our deficit by a few points here, a few points there. With seconds left in the game we tied the score, sending the game into overtime. This time, we took charge, ultimately winning by five, and taking the first round of the playoffs. Afterward the Sun's Katie Douglas acknowledged our effort. "Give credit to Indiana," she said. "They didn't hang their heads."

In winning, we had set the record for the greatest comeback in WNBA playoff history, erasing a deficit of twenty-two points.

In the eastern conference finals we won the first game against the Detroit Shock, putting us within one game of reaching the WNBA Finals for the first time. We had two games to win it, and we squandered our next chance, losing big in Detroit.

And suddenly everything changed. In game three, in the final minute of the second quarter, I jabbed with my right foot, went to take off left, and felt a pain as though someone were kicking me. But as I lay on the floor and looked back, I could see no one was there. They had to wheel me off the court in a wheelchair. At first it was thought to be a sprain, but, no, it was an Achilles tear. I would be off the court for another six months.

Detroit went on to win the final game by sixteen points.

We never know what God has for us. What life we will have and how we will be able to live it. We assume so much day to day about what will happen in the next twenty-four hours, and we so often have this illusion of control. Truth is, we don't control anything; only God does. We just need to live the life he wants for us. And deal with what comes our way.

We were so close to the finals that year. My injury happened at the worst possible time. Losing was a bitter pill.

Another dose of frustration times two. Losing the game and getting injured.

The year 2008 brought us two new faces.

Lin Dunn became our new head coach, replacing Brian Winters, who had led the team into the playoffs successfully but was never able to get us to the finals. Lin had been an assistant coach with the Fever under Brian since 2004.

One *USA Today* sportswriter wrote of Lin Dunn as a cross between Aunt Bee from *The Andy Griffith Show* and Indiana Hoosiers coach Bobby Knight.[1] Lin was the kind of coach who might bake you an apple pie and then throw it across the room at you. She had a folksy charm about her, along with a strong southern drawl, but she could be tough and hard as well.

I confess that back then I wondered if Lin was the right choice for the team. I heard our GM state that our team "needed to go in a different direction," and I felt hiring someone who had been on the staff was too close to the same direction. After three seasons of identical regular season records and almost-but-not-quite getting to the finals, I thought it might be time for the team to bring in someone to shake things up. But time would prove me wrong.

Lin had quite a long legacy in women's basketball, with roots in Tennessee. She graduated from UT Martin and had recruited Pat Summitt to go to school there. And Lin coached a number of college teams before entering the pro ranks. She had experience and success.

The other new face was Katie Douglas.

In the off-season the Fever traded Tamika Whitmore to the Sun for Douglas in one of the biggest trades in WNBA history.

Perhaps Katie's performance in the previous semifinals was the tipping point for the Fever front office. Certainly Katie was a premier player at the top of her game and was highly coveted. Additionally, Katie was an Indianapolis native, one of the reasons she came to the Fever, and she'd be good for local interest, perhaps bolstering attendance at the games. The financial status of some WNBA teams was shaky, and the Fever was one of them. Katie Douglas might help. No doubt it was a strategic acquisition for the team.

But the front office was concerned about the chemistry. Could two all-star players share the same court? Would we constantly be vying for control of the team?

And so it was determined that Katie and I should go to counseling together.

Yes, counseling.

We were sent to a sports psychologist hired by the team. When we first sat down, he looked at us and asked, "Why are you here?" We looked at each other, part smiling, part smirking, and said, "We thought *you* knew."

Katie and I didn't get along very well at first. But the point is that you can't force relationships. You can't manufacture a friendship. A relationship needs to grow naturally, and develop by choice of the two people involved.

How often do we see that in life? We want a relationship to happen, and we want it so badly that we force it. We try to control the other person and strive to manufacture a bond. And that never works. In fact, it messes everything up. A relationship has to develop on its own. Two people need to choose each other in their own way, uncoerced.

The year 2008 was a step back for the Indiana Fever. We finished the regular season just 17–17, although we made it to the playoffs. We faced our archnemesis Detroit Shock in the first round, and we lost in three games.

Frustrating.

In the off-season, Katie went to play for an international team—Galatasaray, a Turkish team in Istanbul. And one day, I got a call. From Katie. She said, "The team here needs a good player. I was thinking of you. Why don't you come here and play on the team with me?"

I did. And in Istanbul, Turkey, that off-season, we developed a friendship.

It felt good to be chosen. From one phone call, a more positive relationship started to form, one that all the team psychology on the planet couldn't manufacture.

When my mom and I moved to Duncanville, the first job she took was at a local ninth-grade school. She had a similar job before we left Illinois and wanted to continue focusing her energy on kids. But after a year, looking ahead, she realized she wanted a job that would give her the flexibility to visit each of her kids. As a result, she pursued a job with American Airlines and could fly most anywhere, anytime. It got to a point where my teammates were just as excited to see my mom as I was, whether we were at a home game or an away game. Mama Catchings was always welcome.

Mom was there in 2008 at the Beijing Olympics. In fact, Mom and Tauja attended each of the three Olympics (Athens, Beijing, and London) I've had the thrill of participating in. Dad and Kenyon came to the one in London.

I was playing for the USA team alongside Sue Bird, Lisa Leslie, Diana Taurasi, Candace Parker, and Kara Lawson, among others. And as a team we were never challenged. We played Australia in the final and won by nearly thirty points. America's dominance in women's basketball would continue, perhaps as a result of the successful college and WNBA programs back home.

I did well in the games, playing good minutes among a wealth of talented players. To Mom, though, I was there, and that was all that mattered. But not even that. She was proud of me for the basketball I played, sure. But I was her little baby girl, and that was all that mattered. She was my cheerleader.

Not just in basketball but in life.

We came back from the Olympics break, and although we made the playoffs, it was a disappointing ending. Yet another off-season to figure out what was going wrong with the Fever. Perhaps the real estate bust and resulting recession of 2007 and 2008 were causing people to pull back on spending. Companies were more conservative in their spending, and sponsorship and partnership opportunities were harder to come by. Nothing was announced, but I could sense that even in our own organization, we needed to have a good—no, *great*—year to keep our team alive.

Winning a championship was on everyone's mind, but getting further than we had, into the conference finals, was a must.

No pressure.

In 2009, Katie and I finally clicked. The Fever had added Briann January in the draft, re-signed Tully Bevilaqua, our energetic point guard and defensive phenom, and got a boost from Tammy Sutton-Brown, who had the year before been named the WNBA's most improved player.

After losing our first two games, we got it together and won our next eleven. We finished with our best regular-season record of 22–12. We earned the first seed in the playoffs, and this time handled our first-round series with Washington rather easily, winning in two games.

Facing the Detroit Shock in the conference finals, we lost the first game. At least subconsciously, we, along with our Indiana fans, were probably thinking, *Here we go again*. But we came back two days later and won by four, setting up a third-game finale.

In the end, we beat Detroit by five points, making our way to the WNBA finals for the first time in franchise history. We would face the Phoenix Mercury in Phoenix for the first two games.

We lost the first game, a close one in overtime that was considered one of the greatest WNBA games of all time. It shattered all kinds of scoring records. We were playing against a team that had won everything just two years before, a team featuring a three-headed scoring monster composed of Diana Taurasi, Cappie Pondexter, and Penny Taylor.

Game two came, and despite the foul troubles and struggle offensively, we were able to come out of it with a win. That meant the series was tied 1–1 and we could return to Indianapolis for the next two games on our home court. We took game three, another close one, winning by just one point. We were just one game away from winning it all.

Indianapolis was buzzing. Game four fell on a Sunday an hour and a half after a Colts home game. The Colts handled business early in the game, so we had fans stripping off their Colts' jerseys to reveal Fever jerseys underneath as they walked the few blocks from the Colts' stadium to Bankers Life Fieldhouse to support us. Suddenly, the building became even more electrified.

Playing game four in front of a home crowd that included Indianapolis Colts Peyton Manning and Reggie Wayne, we struggled. We were down most of the game, and although we fought to stay in the game, we shot miserably in the fourth quarter.

The series tied 2–2, and we would return to Phoenix for a final game.

Again we struggled with our shooting. Our defense was suspect. Fighting from ten points behind a lot of the game, we stayed in it, and with a minute to go, I made a layup that cut Phoenix's lead to just two points. As we played out the last sixty seconds, we fouled to force Phoenix to make free throws.

And they made them all—six shots in the final minute—and we went down 94–86.

It was hugely disappointing to get so close and yet not win it all. Katie was devastated because she'd had a bad night shooting.

And yet, a lot of people considered the five-game series some of the best WNBA basketball ever. Our two teams showcased the best offensive team against the best defensive team and we took it down to the last minute of the last game. The Indiana Fever had played great basketball and competed well at the highest level.

And the fans had come out, supporting the team and saving the franchise. Sometime later, our team owners came out with a comment that "the Indiana Fever would remain in Indianapolis."

One of the responsibilities that came with my increasing leadership role with the Fever was off the court. I was asked more and more to do public speaking. Of course, at first I was uncomfortable doing it, given my childhood experiences with hearing loss and a mild speech problem. Not to mention my natural shyness. Getting up in front of people and talking is a far cry from that quiet solitude by the side of a nameless Tennessee lake.

But my sister, Tauja, ever my motivator, convinced me I could do it, encouraging me and coaching me in public speaking.

Years before, during my first off-season while I was still rehabbing, the Fever's community relations director, Lori Satterfield, had asked me to start doing some public speaking. Initially I told her no, because I knew I'd be terrible at it. She and Tauja both encouraged me. Lori said, "You can do it. We can create a script that you can say verbatim. Each time you do the speech, you'll get more and more comfortable, and eventually it'll come naturally. You'll be great."

So we talked about what I'd say. Lori had already come up with an acronym for FEVER—"For Every Victory Earns Respect." And we developed a speaking script around that using what I knew—basketball—to create my message.

It worked. We started the school tour with my FEVER speech, and while I was a bit rough at first, the more I did it, the easier it became. Lori would be at each of the schools to listen to my delivery. Afterward she would coach me on what I could do better. I became more comfortable and a lot more fluid.

In time, I would experience the ultimate compliment: kids coming up to me on the street, saying, "You came to my school and spoke to us. That was so great!" And they'd remember my speech, reciting back to me the acronym—"For Every Victory Earns Respect."

In those moments, it's all worth it.

And no one really knew the fear I had inside in those moments, the butterflies in my stomach and the disastrous thoughts that floated through my head. But before every speech, then and now, I say a prayer to help me get through.

One thing that became more and more important to me when I moved to Indy was church. I found a church called New Life Worship Center, and I quickly got myself immersed in the Word. I was attracted to the church's powerful music and its teaching. It was a church firmly built on the Word of God.

I attended New Life as often as I could. Sometimes the Fever's games, practices, or travel made it impossible for me to be there on Sundays, but if I missed, I would catch the service online later.

Sundays when I was there, I'd enjoy the music—contemporary, powerful, a wall of sound that praised God and allowed me to sing to him. And I'd eagerly listen to the sermon by up-and-coming Pastor John Ramsey, opening up a notebook I kept for sermon notes and jotting down his main points and Scriptures.

Many of my friends and even family members talk about my faith as if it's like one more tough self-discipline thing I do. But, to me, it's not about discipline. It's about being in the presence of God himself. It's about hearing God speak to me. Being in church is what I want to do and what is important to me. It feeds my soul.

After I'd attended New Life a while, the pastor's wife, Alicia, came up to me and said if ever I needed to talk, she would be happy to be available to me. She had a sense of the potential challenges I faced being something of a *celebrity*. "Sometimes you might need a friend to confide in," she said. "I gotcha."

That began a friendship that continues to this day. Alicia is a friend, yes, but she is much more too. She's a mentor. Someone apart from my family and my basketball world who can reflect the light of God's Word into my life.

Most of all, Alicia has given me wise guidance about relationships. At one point, I found myself interested in a guy I met while traveling to a game. He and I struck up a conversation, and I liked him. When I came home, I continued to stay in touch with him, and I also confided this to Alicia.

She listened as a friend does, but later did something she had never done before—she googled the guy. What popped up was a picture of him with some other people he probably shouldn't have been with, or rather that I shouldn't be with. When Alicia and I got together again, she said, "Tamika, do what you want to, but I'm just saying this guy's not it."

I didn't end that relationship right there and then, but eventually I did, and I told Alicia later, "You know, that guy's just not it."

From 2009 through 2011, the Fever's regular season record would be consistent—winning twenty-one or twenty-two games each year. Good records, all knocking on the door of a championship. But in 2010, though we made it to the playoffs, we lost in the first round to New York in three games.

Following the 2009 season, and in the beginning of 2010, the Fever acquired Shavonte Zellous from Tulsa. Shavonte, a do-it-all guard, would prove to be a significant contributor to the team in coming years, another piece of a puzzle that was being assembled. But we lost someone too—our starting power forward, Ebony Hoffman, to the Los Angeles Sparks. And that was sad for me because Ebony and her husband, Ron, had become my best friends on the team.

In 2011 we reached the playoffs once again. The Fever had become one of the stronger and more consistent teams in the league, and while we might be considered an elite team, we weren't yet thought of as being one of the teams at the very top. Not yet. We hadn't consistently advanced further in the playoffs. But it was becoming clear that we had the talent to do better.

And we thought we *could* do better. We'd finished tied for first in our division, and we had had good records against the better teams. We thought this year we could advance to the finals.

We faced New York in the eastern conference semis, and we won both our home games, advancing to the conference finals. We'd done it.

In the finals, though, we faced the Atlanta Dream. While in the regular season we'd bested a lot of strong teams, the Dream had had our number. Though they finished third in our division that year, we faced them four times in the regular season—and lost all four games.

When we won the first game of the series, 83–74, it really looked good. But game two was a blowout, with one of Atlanta's guards shooting lights out from the outside.

My dad was present for game three back in Indianapolis, and while I never allow myself to be distracted by family and friends who are at courtside, I was aware of his presence. After years of pro basketball success, he and I were still butting heads. I'd come to understand that Dad meant well. He was there, watching, rooting for me, and that counted for a lot. But at the same time, he wanted to coach me, just as he had coached me when I was a girl and when I was in college. And even when I reached the WNBA, he was still trying to coach me. He would still talk to me after a game, tell me what I could have done differently, what I could do better. "You should be taking the shot here. Don't pass it off like that, Mika."

Often, I know, he is pushing me to step up as a premier player. He wants me to take the lead. He argues that I need to take the shot.

I know Dad wants me to be the best I can be.

We lost game three, at home, against Atlanta. Katie Douglas shot well, but it wasn't a good game for me. We wouldn't advance to the finals.

Immediately after the game, I wondered what Dad was thinking. I was sure he'd have comments. It was all very confusing. At the end of the 2011 regular season the WNBA had voted me Most Valuable Player. And yet that somehow wasn't enough.

Part 5

HARMONY

Balls bouncing . . .
Kids playing . . .
Nets swishing . . .
Crowds cheering . . .
This is my harmony . . .
I hear it.
I see it.
I live it.
I feel it.
I AM IT!

15

WINNING

"We have to match Catchings's intensity. She's playing so much harder than anybody on the floor."

Cheryl Reeve, head coach, Minnesota Lynx,
at halftime of WNBA Finals, Game Three

I understand the need for teams to shuffle the pieces, look
for the players who will provide the edge for the next season,
and try to tinker with the chemistry—especially when the
mix of talent didn't get you to the championship the year
before. But I also think teams sometimes don't have the patience for the chemistry to come together, and by bringing
too many new players into the mix, they wind up starting
the chemistry clock all over again.

But for the Fever in 2012, the changes were minimal, and
the opportunity was there for us to put it all together. We
had a good feeling about this.

Of course, every year in the beginning you have a good feeling about your chances.

I can't say that I hadn't started thinking about my career as a whole and my future. I didn't dwell on it, but some thoughts had started to cross my mind. This marked my eleventh year in the WNBA. I was at the top of my game, feeling good, anticipating more years of playing time. But eleven years in the WNBA is a long time. And I knew it couldn't last forever.

The average length of a WNBA career is fairly short. Some have done the math and figured the average is between three and four years. Actually, that sounds long to me. I've seen so many come out of college and last only a year or two.

Some of that has to do with injuries, and some of that has to do with life choices and the generally low pay scale in women's professional basketball. But another factor is the competitive nature of the league itself. In 2012, the WNBA had twelve teams with eleven players per team—only 132 roster spots. That means in the college draft each year, it's usually the first-round picks that stick and make a difference.

And for a veteran—for a second-, third-, or fourth-year player—you're not only competing for a roster spot against the players drafted in your draft year, but all the first-round players drafted in years since. Because of the smaller size of the WNBA and the roster size of basketball teams, the flood of college talent each year squeezes through a very narrow funnel for starting spots in the WNBA.

And veteran players have to be at the top of their game to survive. One case in point, although Katie Douglas and I were Fever players on the All-Star team in 2011, other teams had three or more All-Stars representing them. In fact, the Minnesota Lynx had four of their five starters on the All-Star team in 2011.

It is a league of elite players, and the competition is relentless.

It was way too early for me to retire, but after ten years in the league, I began to realize that my future chances at a championship might be pretty limited.

I knew in 2012 we could be close to being competitive at the highest level. More than ever, I wanted us to win it all.

Before the 2012 season started, Coach Lin Dunn called me to lunch to discuss a "change" she wanted to make for the season. We met up and Lin said, "Tamika, I want to move you from playing the 3 to the 4."

All the positions on the court have numbers. A small forward or in some cases the third guard is a 3. A power forward is a 4. I'd been used to playing the small forward position, which is the most versatile role on the court, allowing me to move freely, sometimes bring the ball up, often slide around the perimeter, and sometimes sneak inside for a layup.

But Coach had an idea that I could be more effective in the 4 position, as a power forward. She said she needed me more in the middle of the floor. She felt that in the small forward position I was sometimes stuck in the corners and not involved in enough plays. As a power forward, she felt, I had the strength to muscle in close, but also the quickness to take advantage of bigger, slower bodies inside. And what's more, she reasoned, I would be in a better position to grab rebounds.

I wasn't so sure. To change my position at this stage was a big shift, for me and others. It sounded to me like it was restricting me from the freedom of the small forward position.

Then Coach Dunn said something else. "I want you to be a *point* forward," she said. "I think you can bring the ball up the court, start the play, then slide down to the post as power forward. Their power forward won't move high and play you when you bring the ball up, and you're stronger than their guards. It'll give us a big advantage."

Now that sounded good.

We started the 2012 season solidly, winning our first four games. Katie came out in the first game and was high scorer with twenty-one points. I would pour in twenty-two and twenty-five points in the next two games respectively. We won by good margins. It felt good, promising.

But then we went on a losing streak, falling short in the next three contests. Our first game against the Connecticut Sun in June was for me one of the more frustrating games that season—I scored thirty-one points, and we still lost. Less than a week later, we played them again—and lost again, although in overtime.

The Sun would prove to be the elite team in our conference that year. If we wanted to get through the playoffs, chances were we would need to go through them.

The WNBA year starts sometime in late April or early May and ends in October. There's a break in the middle—in July/August—which most years is when the All-Star game is scheduled. And every other year, the league breaks for a month to provide time for players to compete at the World Championships or the Olympics.

My third Olympics, in London, gave me a chance for reflection. I am so blessed by God to be able to represent my country and play at such a high level. Being in London for another run at the Olympic gold was not the same-old, same-old by any means. No Olympics is ever that. But it was an experience I'd been through before, twice, and I knew the ropes.

There's never enough time at the Olympics to do much, but this time through, I had a different perspective. Maybe it was my work with young people in Indianapolis through my Catch the Stars Foundation, or just my view now that I was a little older. But I tried to live in the moment and enjoy the time together with my teammates and such a great group of people.

The Olympics, despite all the competition, brings people together. We aren't dozens of different nations, really. We're just people, young people, who have the same kinds of feelings, thoughts, worries, and joys. We're all driven to be the best and we've been trained to be able to deliver . . . when it counts.

While the United States was the usual favorite in women's basketball, having dominated the sport for so many years, there was no such thing as a guaranteed gold. For us, this would be an Olympic year without Lisa Leslie and with a number of new players. And, as always, we were the team with the bull's-eye on our back—the team every other team was playing over their heads to beat.

We nonetheless beat our opponents all the way through the quarters and semis. We would face the surprising France in the gold medal game. They had pulled an upset over Russia in the quarters. And France featured an outstanding guard—Céline Dumerc—who could be a threat.

I was told later that NBA commissioner David Stern was in the crowd. As was Kobe Bryant.

France played us even in the first few minutes. We were missing easy shots, forcing the game. Sure, Bird said later that we weren't nervous but simply trying to win too quickly. I think that was right. That might sound arrogant—I don't mean it that way—but we were too aggressive and too urgent to play well.

But then we settled in, relaxed, and our shots started to fall in. After that, they couldn't match us. We led by nearly thirty points at the half, and eventually cruised to an easy win.

So it was another gold medal—although no gold medal is *just another* gold medal. And maybe it was an even more touching awards ceremony this time, with the *Chariots of Fire* theme song playing in the background as medals were handed out. Then, standing tall, hand over heart, for the national anthem. It's really something to stand there at the Olympics while "The Star Spangled Banner" is playing. You can't help but have tears in your eyes. You can't help but be grateful and thankful for all the opportunities that have allowed you to get here.

The WNBA second half started the third week in August.

Back home, we knew we had to do better. Our first half record of 10–7 wasn't nearly the pace we needed to set. We'd been losing to teams we knew would be our toughest competition in the playoffs.

If we got to the playoffs.

Returning to the States, we would play seven games in the last two weeks of August. We won six out of the seven. And it was the *way* we started winning that was the key. Each night a different high scorer would step up. Sometimes it was Katie, sometimes me, but also sometimes Briann January. The phrase "letting the game come to you" is a cliché in all of sports, but there's a lot of truth in it. You need time to figure out the other team's strategy, to see what they are throwing at you and what they will do in certain situations you throw at them. Eventually you can see how the other team is trying to shut you down, and by doing that, who they are leaving open. That's when the game "comes to you" as a team—you "solve" the defense and then go to the shooter the other team is leaving open.

Sometimes people ask, "Why do you often start a game so slowly?" Yes, we often play another team pretty even for the first few minutes, or even fall behind at the beginning of the game. Well, that's why—we're figuring out what the other team is doing. We're waiting for the game to come to us. We're exploring alternative options and going to other shooters—and sometimes it takes a while to find out what works.

I think this is true in life also. We sometimes go through periods when we feel like we're just slogging through life, taking a step forward, and then a step back. We're living life "even," not getting anywhere. But I think those are also times when we learn a lot—about ourselves, about being tested, about overcoming opposition. And then God brings the game of life to us. He says, "Now's your chance." And in those moments, you become God's go-to shooter. And you need to be ready to follow his lead.

For the Fever that fall, we were learning that the game didn't rest just on me to play D and make shots, or on Katie to get open and score. Others could step up as well, be the go-to shooter, ready when the game came to them.

By the end of August we'd turned our record around—to 16–8. It became clear that, unless we totally collapsed in September, we'd be in the playoffs. But we needed to do better against three teams that had had our number—Atlanta, Connecticut, and Minnesota.

We played ten games in September. We won six and lost four. But one loss was against Atlanta, another against Connecticut. And we lost two to Minnesota.

So the good news was that we made the playoffs.

The bad news was that, as it turned out, in the playoffs we would need to beat Atlanta, Connecticut, and Minnesota—in that order.

But the good thing about the playoffs is that all teams start from scratch. It's a new beginning, a chance for the best teams to play each other, and for, perhaps, a new team to emerge triumphant.

But we'd have to solve teams who had been our toughest competition all year. And it didn't start well.

The Atlanta Dream jumped out in the first game of the conference semis and took it to us.

They came out fast, scoring the first eleven points. We were beaten on the inside, a rarity for our team, and our three-point shooting, usually our strength, was flat. Meanwhile the Dream's Angel McCoughtry, the leading scorer in the league that season, shot lights out.

We'd need to win game two to stay alive and game three to move on. As they say, "Win or go home!"

I knew I had to do better. The team needed both Katie and me to perform, whether or not the Dream was trapping the two of us. We just had to determine in the flow of the game which of us they couldn't double-team.

In game two, I became that one. Katie drew the defense to her, giving me, as well as Briann January, room to work.

We played tight the first quarter, and although we had a one-point lead with just three seconds left, the Dream's Ketia Swanier launched a last-minute Hail-Mary three-pointer from half-court that went in. Likewise, in the second quarter, we played close, trading leads. There were fourteen lead changes in the first half alone. We played hard, but just couldn't break it open. We went into halftime down by two and our season hanging in the balance.

We took charge in the third quarter. Briann scored from inside and outside, winding up with twenty-four points. I scored twenty-five and had thirteen rebounds. We ran away with it and won by fifteen points. We earned a chance to stay alive in the playoffs by getting to a third game.

I remember that game very well because of one person seated in the first row. One very special person. Coach Pat Summitt.

The previous year, in May, Pat Summitt visited the Mayo Clinic to look into a series of memory lapses. The diagnosis was early onset dementia, Alzheimer's. While the disease was just in its beginning stages, it had started to affect Pat's performance as a coach. Later in 2012 she would announce her retirement.

When my mom drove me to Knoxville in August 1997, she did so knowing that Pat Summitt would take care of me. And she did. Pat was not only a legendary, tough-as-nails coach to me; she was like my second mom. And most every young lady entering the basketball program at Tennessee would say the same thing.

And now Pat Summitt was sitting at courtside watching me play. Those laser eyes had dimmed a little, and she looked a little more frail. But her presence and smile meant everything to me.

That win in Atlanta bought us another chance, game three, back in Indianapolis. And we were resolved not to let this one slip away.

It was a total team effort. The Dream focused on defending me a bit more, but then Katie really took off, scoring a game-high twenty-five points. Briann, again, played tough, and Erlana Larkins was strong in the middle. We were ahead most of the game, sometimes by just a few points, and the Dream tied us for a moment in the third quarter.

But we pulled away in the final quarter and won by eleven. We beat Atlanta, one of our toughest opponents all year, and we advanced to the conference finals against number one seeded Connecticut Sun.

The series started with another loss against the Sun, but game two was a classic.

I bounced back from being shut down in the first game and had something like seventeen points in the first quarter.

But the Sun, featuring MVP Tina Charles and Olympic star Asjha Jones, played us tough. With twenty seconds left in the game, the teams were tied. The Sun's Allison Hightower was at the line to shoot a free throw.

Once again, we were playing for our survival. If we lost, we would go home, our efforts to reach and win a championship thwarted yet again.

Hightower missed her free throw, and I grabbed the rebound, quickly firing an outlet pass up to Briann. Briann raced toward the basket with just a few seconds left and slid in for a layup. But she missed it.

Erlana was able to tip the rebound back to Briann, who desperately shoveled it out to Shavonte Zellous. Shavonte, with just one second left on the clock, jumped and released the ball.

And it went in. We won by two points. Once again we scrambled and clawed our way into the third and final game of a series.

In game three we would face our greatest test.

Just ten minutes into the first quarter, Katie, going up for a jump shot, came down hard on her left foot, and it buckled at the ankle. She had to be carted off the court.

The rest of us were stunned, but we knew we had to step up. I knew I had to pick up my game, and I did. And so did the rest of the Fever. We went ahead by nine in the second quarter, and never let go, winning finally by sixteen points.

Some people wonder how it is that when a star player goes down, the team sometimes performs better. There are all kinds of theories about that, and frankly, I don't know. We won that game, I think, because suddenly everyone knew we had to make up for the considerable loss of Katie's scoring.

When bad things happen, sometimes that's an opportunity for something better. It wasn't what we'd planned, maybe, but it sets up a new situation that we might be able to thrive in. I think it's when we have a particular need, and we face our sudden weakness honestly and directly, that God can do more with us.

It's because, in our need, we rely on him more.

I truly believe it's only when you get close to the top of the mountain that you realize how rare it is to get that close—and how important it is to make that last effort and climb to the top.

We had made the finals in 2009, losing in a long, tough championship series. And though we had every expectation we'd return to the finals the next year and the year after that, it didn't happen. Getting to the finals is a rare thing. We'd been here before and fallen short. Who knows when we would get here again?

We had to do it this time.

We would face the Minnesota Lynx in a best of five series. Minnesota had won the WNBA championship the year before. They would win again a year later. In 2012, they were the odds-on favorite to beat us. Not only were they deeply talented but they had a winner's swagger. They, and everyone else, felt they would pretty much sweep the series against us.

We weren't intimidated. Erlana Larkins said it best: "We've made it to this point, what's there to fear? We know they're the defending champions and they're going to bring their 'A' game . . . . So what, they're the defending champs? We're here to take one." Those are ambitious words, coming from a team that would be playing without Katie Douglas. But they weren't just trash talk. We believed we could beat Minnesota. But our biggest challenge would be to do it without Katie Douglas. For once, we were the team to steal game one. We shut down Maya Moore, and our bench contributed mightily. I scored twenty, but it was Erlana and Briann who picked up the slack from the injured Katie.

Minnesota came out with a rush in the second half and even took a lead, but we pulled ahead after that and eventually won the game by six.

Interviewed later, I said, "We are not here to just be in the finals. We are here for a great opportunity, and both teams, we both want it bad. So every game is going to be just like this game. It's going to be tough, it's going to be hard-nosed."

Game two was exactly that, featuring a technical foul on Lindsay Whalen after a hard steal and a subsequent technical on Lynx coach Cheryl Reeve, upset with the call. But that just seemed to motivate them. For us, we would lose our second sharpshooter, Jeanette Pohlen, to an ACL injury.

We led the game by ten in the second quarter, but Minnesota came back by the half, and then started to run away with it in the second half. We lost the game by twelve.

Tough to lose, but it was good to get at least a split in Minneapolis. Now the games would be played in front of our home fans in Indianapolis. And that home field advantage, believe me, would be a real plus. Our fans were the best, and we fueled off them.

However, what wasn't encouraging was the injury to Jeanette, adding to our injury woes, and the way the Lynx, especially Maya and Lindsay, took over the game in the second half.

Game three in Indianapolis turned out to be bizarre.

I came out playing hard and piling up points. We led at the quarter by about five. Good, but still close. But then as the game came to me, and as the Lynx swarmed to shut me down, I was able to pass it off to my teammates. And, oh my, did they deliver! Shavonte came out of nowhere and started sinking threes. As the Lynx came out to defend her, she fed it to Briann, who powered in for layups inside. It was beautiful. We ran away with it.

At one point in the third quarter we were winning 70–33. I'm told that's the largest lead by any team in WNBA finals history. Some said the Lynx just played badly. I don't know. I think we just put it all together in ten or fifteen shining minutes in game three. Shavonte scored thirty points. Wow.

We won big, but more important, we had asserted the best of ourselves, and given the Lynx something to think about for game four—for them, potentially an elimination game.

We had an opportunity to do something that had never before been done in Indiana women's basketball. The question was, would we rise to the challenge?

This was not "another championship." If we won, it would be the Fever's first. It would be the culmination of more than ten years of building the franchise. It was important to the city of Indianapolis and the state of Indiana. It was important to the WNBA—to have another team climb the mountain and rise to the peak, not one of a select few who had won a lot in the past.

We were playing without Katie Douglas and Jeanette Pohlen. We were playing game four against the strongest team in the WBNA, who had won the championship twice in years leading up to this. We knew, despite our blowout of them the previous game, they'd put that behind them quickly and would be a formidable challenge. We had everything stacked against us.

Of course my mom and dad were there, as well as my sister and brother. Dad was the sought-after interview, as always. It was reported that he said my success exceeded any satisfaction he had from his eleven-year pro career.

We came out strong in the first quarter. The Lynx pressured me, but as in game three, other teammates rose up to score and rebound. At the half, we were up by five. But we knew the last twenty minutes of the game would be hard-fought, and we'd face peaks and valleys.

There are times in sports when you develop a hyper-focus and it's as if you can sense everything on the court happening all at once, almost in slow motion. You can sense the plays developing and the other team scrambling to cover, and you can pass the ball to the right person at the right time or take the shot yourself with great ease. And I think, for me, years of questions about leadership and being a team player and taking the shot came into great clarity. And suddenly I knew when to shoot and when to pass and how to be the leader for our team.

We led by just three toward the end of the third quarter, and the Lynx kept our leads to single digits throughout. Shavonte, again, was shooting well, and so was Erin Phillips. But our strength all game was our relentless defense. We kept pressure on the Lynx, and forced them to take tough shots.

With a minute to play, we were up by eight. It looked good, but as any basketball fan knows, a game can be lost in a hurry on the free throw line.

But then suddenly the minute was almost gone. We were up by seven. Coach Lin took a time-out she didn't have to take. But she substituted Katie Douglas, still hobbling on her healing ankle, so she could get into the championship game. The Indy crowd roared, and it brought tears to many eyes.

The clock's final seconds ticked down, and then—the game was over.

We were the 2012 WNBA Champions.

16

LIFE

Do not be conformed to this world, but be transformed by the renewing of your mind, that you may prove what is that good and acceptable and perfect will of God.

Romans 12:2 NKJV

". . . they rallied behind my good friend, whom I've had the pleasure of being on the court with (and she took it easy on me!), Tamika Catchings, MVP, who can now add a WNBA championship to her NCAA championship, three-time Olympic gold medalist. . . ."

I would never have imagined that the person speaking about me would be President Barack Obama. I would never have imagined that I'd be handing the president of the United States a commemorative basketball, hat, and jersey. I would never have imagined that this little girl with a hearing loss, bullied in school, would some twenty years later be standing tall in the White House, being lauded with her other teammates.

In fact, this was not the first time I'd met the president. In 2008, during his presidential campaign, Obama visited Kokomo, Indiana, and participated in a three-on-three game. As I was still rehabbing from my Achilles tear, I was called in to referee. I'd also been invited to two State of the Union addresses—one for George Bush and one for Barack Obama. I have to say, the business of government fascinates and intrigues me. Someone once asked me an interesting question: "If you could be Invisible Woman for a day, what would you do?" I said, "I'd go to the White House and see what they got going on."

I'd been privileged to be a part of Michelle Obama's Let's Move! Tour early in 2012, before our championship season. Let's Move! is an initiative to counter the problem of childhood obesity. It dovetails well with my Catch the Stars Foundation, which emphasizes "literacy, fitness, and mentoring."

It was a very special honor to be at the White House that day with my teammates and Lin Dunn, and to be acknowledged by the president for what the team had done, for the championship we'd won. The president talked about how women's basketball had done so much for girls growing up and giving them a sense of possibility. He mentioned that what we'd done had empowered women. So the experience that day gave me a sense of how our championship represented not only Indianapolis and Indiana but all of America.

But as affirming and wonderful as that was, I knew something deep inside. This, even this, is not what really matters.

Our championship set Indiana on fire. It was the state's first professional basketball title since 1973. The men's team, the Indiana Pacers, had won it several times in the old ABA league early in the seventies, but never since that time. Indiana, proud of both its professional teams, could now boast a championship.

Indianapolis scheduled a parade, but weather was predicted to be so bad they had to cancel it. Instead they scheduled a celebration in the arena—Banker's Life Fieldhouse.

The place was packed. The atmosphere was charged.

I got congratulations tweets from LeBron James, Dwayne Wade, and Peyton Manning.

The state's political VIPs were there, and some spoke. So did GM Kelly Krauskopf, who had taken a chance on me some ten years earlier; she said she felt she could finally breathe after a decade of building the team.

Coach Lin Dunn then spoke, saying that Atlanta, Connecticut, and Minnesota had never seen the level of defense we had played. She introduced each of the Fever players, one by one, and eventually got to Katie Douglas. Katie, was, of course, the hometown girl, a big favorite in the city and state. Katie got a huge ovation.

Then Lin said, "Let's see . . . who have I forgot?"

The crowd roared and began chanting, "MVP . . . MVP . . . MVP . . ."

I got up to speak. Just a few words—and I don't even remember what I said. Well, I remember one thing: "This has been a journey like no other."

I'm sure some think that's a cliché or trite, and maybe it is, for some. But for me this was very special. This represented overcoming so much in my life, working hard, fighting to be the best. It was about our hanging in there through ten years of ups and down, climbing the mountain each year, only to be disappointed. It meant getting to the final ascent, and then pulling ourselves up to the very top, finally able to look around to see what we'd accomplished.

It was wonderful. It was a dream realized.

But still I knew that's not what really matters.

In early 2013 I re-upped my contract with the Fever. By re-signing, I knew I would finish my pro career with them. It mattered to me that they seemed intent on winning it all during my final years there, but I was leaning toward staying with them anyway. Loyalty is important to me. I wanted to be loyal to them. Plus, I couldn't imagine playing for any other organization outside of Pacers Sports & Entertainment.

Our goal in 2013, of course, was to repeat as champions. Our team remained intact from 2012 to 2013, unusual for the WNBA. But then again, why tamper with success? We were a strong shooting team, and we managed ball possessions really well. We also excelled on defense.

We came out in 2013, losing six of our first seven games. While we didn't want to make excuses, the reality was that we faced a number of injuries right off the bat. Katie Douglas had had chronic back issues throughout her career, and after two games, she was out with a bulging disc. Center Jessica Davenport suffered a stress fracture that knocked her out for the year. Erin Phillips was out for a number of games with a knee injury. Jeanette Pohlen, after coming back from a torn ACL, tore her Achilles and would be out for the season.

We would come back from that miserable start and win seven in a row. So we *could* put it together. But it was a year when sometimes we just didn't. We made the playoffs that year, but finished fourth in our conference with a losing record. And while we advanced through the conference semis of the playoffs, we'd lose in the next round to Atlanta.

I was becoming more aware that my playing days were nearing an end. Not because I felt I was declining—not at all. But because I knew that certain physical realities and age would prompt a decline eventually, and I didn't want to play at less than my best.

My college education in sports management led me to think about leading a team myself someday. I've never really wanted to coach. But I had once thought I wanted to own a WNBA team. However, recently, my thoughts had changed. Owners didn't do much in building teams—that's what general managers do. And so my focus shifted to being a GM someday.

I had watched our general manager and president, Kelly Krauskopf, build the team from the beginning. I felt she and I had developed a special bond. I knew she had taken a big chance drafting me as an injured player in 2002, and over the years she had built the franchise around me. I had played up to that challenge, and I knew she valued me for that.

I had watched her through the years, slowly building the Fever, trying to get the right pieces and fit them together. And while she had done a great job, eventually winning it all in 2012, she was well aware of how rare that was. No one could predict injuries. But she could bring players together who had chemistry, and whose styles of play complemented each other.

I'm not saying I wanted *her* job, but I could see myself doing the kind of work she does. I've learned a lot from watching her.

Obviously I felt it important to stay connected to basketball. At the point I couldn't play anymore, I wanted to be in the game at some level. Maybe that would be someday as a general manager, I didn't know.

Basketball had been my life. It was my dad's career. It had been the centerpiece of my family's life.

And yet, for all of that, I knew that even basketball is not what really matters.

Kelly made a lot of changes in the 2013–2014 off-season.

For one thing, Katie Douglas left the Fever, going back to the Connecticut Sun. Katie had suffered a lot from back problems, and was likely approaching the end of her career. But she had played with Connecticut before coming to the Fever, and they offered her a good deal to return.

Meanwhile, Kelly had two first-round draft picks and brought Natasha Howard and Natalie Achonwa, both forwards, to the Fever. Marissa Coleman, a small forward, was acquired from the Los Angeles Sparks. All in all, six new players would be on our roster. We would complement them with returning veterans Shavonte Zellous, Briann January, and me, but it was a substantially new team.

And then, I suffered an injury. What started out as some tingling in my knee and feeling a weakness when I tried to push off of it ended up being a pinched nerve in my back and would cause me to miss the first part of the season. Injections and rest were the prescription. I don't do rest very well, but I had to sit out and take care of myself.

I returned on July 10, two-thirds into the season. We played the Connecticut Sun, and it was a strange feeling for me to square off against Katie Douglas.

The Fever made the playoffs, finishing second in the conference. We beat Washington in the semis, but lost to Chicago in the conference finals, once again missing a trip to the championship game.

In October 2014 I released a statement announcing the end date for my playing career. I would play two more seasons with the Fever, and hopefully, compete in the Olympics one last time in 2016.

In a TV interview, I said, "I will be retiring in 2016, Lord willing, if my body holds up. Although I plan to step away as a player, that is not to say I'll step away from the game, hopefully. I am so thankful and blessed to have had an opportunity to play the game I have loved for so long. God has truly blessed me with an amazing playing career, and now it's time to start transitioning to what he has for me beyond the lines of the basketball floor."

In 2015 I started learning how to shoot . . . all over again.

Eight years ago I began working with a renowned shooting coach, Marvin "Doc" Harvey, who studied the form of great basketball shooters, developed the theory and practice of shooting, and helped the likes of Michael Jordan with his shot.

For all of my experience in shooting and my success doing it on the court, I knew I could do better. Over the years, I have watched Kobe shoot, as well as Kevin Durant and Stephen Curry—all of them using their own classic form in shooting a basketball. My shot was a homegrown technique, one that had worked for me in a way through the years, but had problems. I knew that.

I told Doc that when I looked at Bryant, Durant, and Curry, their shooting looked so effortless and natural. "For me," I admitted, "I have a grimace on my face. It's like a shot for me is just such hard work!"

Doc Harvey replied, "That was the most profound thing you said to me. Okay, let's get the shot right."

So the transition that started almost eight years ago has shifted into a different phase. Now there's been an increased focus in different aspects of my shot with the overall goal to go out on top being the best ME that I can be. And, man, it's hard. You start playing without the ball, working on form only. It's pantomime, learning the proper sequence of body movements and motions.

I learned that, in a game, as you get tired, your shot changes. You use your arms throughout the game, and they get tired. You start missing shots. Instead, you're supposed to use your legs.

My shooting training with Doc emphasized how balanced movements throughout my whole body caused me to shoot more efficiently. The teachings included the timing of the hands and feet working together, along with the rhythm of the upper and lower body movements. These parts were repeated thousands of times until they became habit. When all parts were working together the only thing I had to focus on was my fingers directing the ball in a straight line, the proper arc, and back spin on the ball.

And if you do this right, it explodes out the same way every time.

But to get to that point, you have to practice endlessly. Over and over. And for the longest time, it feels unnatural. And when you're actually shooting the ball, you miss the shot at first.

The toughest thing for a player is to miss shots.

And the temptation is to go back to your old way of doing things to sink the basket. But you have to avoid that, fight against that instinct, and practice the discipline of doing it the right way, using the right form, following the sequence of shooting that ultimately works best.

How often do we do things our way, our old-life way, and while we think we get away with that just fine, we aren't really achieving the life God wants for us?

His way of living life is what's best for us. But sometimes we have to go through his discipline to get there. We have to relearn how to live, get away from bad habits, and practice the life he has for us. It's like an infant learning to walk for the first time.

But ultimately, it's better. God's way is always better.

17

TRANSITION

There's only one way to go from here . . . forward.

Tamika

I'm writing this late in 2015, a year away from life without ball, and God has shown me his better way with all the opportunities and people he continues to bring into my life. What my life has taught me (and the people closest to me have taught me this as well) is that I can be a little stubborn and strong-willed. But on the flipside, the positives include my passion, my love, my selflessness, the warrior inside of me, the discipline, the self-motivation, and the work ethic. So the challenge ahead will be whether I can relinquish some control of life so that I can let someone else into it.

I think I can. It's the lesson I've also had to learn about God and me. It will take work in my relationships and the

245

next phase of my life, I know. But no one ever accused me of not working hard.

There's so much to accomplish, and I truly believe these fourteen years I've played basketball are just the tip of the iceberg for where God has me next. I'm eager to see where my life and all the items on my "to do" list end up.

- Get married
- Have kids
- Be a general manager in basketball
- Inspire, motivate, and encourage others

It's time to move on to the next thing God has for me. Like I always speak about, life is all about new goals. When you reach one, you enjoy the success, but you continue to set out to do new things. Never get content with doing just one thing, or reaching just one goal. Your success propels you to the next goal—short or long term.

So the real test for all my relationships will be my retirement as an active player. Which ones stand firm based on the true foundation that has been set, and which ones dwindle away based only on basketball.

That, we will soon see.

I envision this scene in my head with our Catch the Stars youth basketball camps here in Indianapolis:

Some of the kids are here, but the basketballs haven't yet arrived. I walk into the gym and start talking to them. Some of them talk with ease, and others just stare in admiration. They're excited that I'm there—a real-life basketball star.

Over time I have all of them talking, laughing, and joking. To me, it's always been fun to watch kids gradually come out of their shells and allow me to see the "real" them. They are so full of life and potential.

Across the way, on the court, I see a girl all alone, maybe ten years old.

I turn back to the kids around me. Some tell me how they won their game on a city playground court the day before. Some tell me about their siblings and parents.

I love being around kids.

I look up and see that same girl on the court. I watch her more closely this time. She's still just there all by herself, but now she is moving on the court, running, darting, dodging, and weaving. Practicing. Perhaps pretending to be a star forward in the WNBA, she pretends to dribble an invisible basketball. She drives up the court, stops, then jumps. And shoots, her arms extending above her head, her fingers stretched.

And I know what she hears.

The roar of a crowd. The rush of the game. And the mesmerizing swish of a basketball falling through the net.

I look at that girl, so like myself years ago, and I wonder about her life ahead. Her relationships. Her family. And if she hears God in her life.

You see, that's what really matters.

ACKNOWLEDGMENTS

It's weird to write a story on your life before the next phase of your life has begun, but it's also cool to be able to write about all of the amazing things that have happened in my life thus far. God has been so GREAT to me.

In writing my story, I wanted to talk about my struggle, my faith, and just the journey to becoming me. I couldn't have done this without the help of Baker Publishing Group, Ken Petersen, my family, friends, coaches, teachers, University of Tennessee, Pacers Sports & Entertainment, my fans, and just so many people that unbeknownst to them have helped push and motivate me to always be my best. I'm so thankful for God putting the right people in my life at the right time. I've gone through the heartbreaks of relationships and have lost friends along the way, but he's always provided me with an avenue to keep on pushing forward.

This book finishes after a super run with my team all the way to Game 5 in the WNBA Finals. I think it's fair to say that we were never expected to make it that far. But, with the determination, willpower, grit, and pure heart that we had as a team, we made it and we showed people what it means to be all in and to give everything you have, every moment you have. That drive will be something that I'll never forget, and those in the basketball world will never forget too.

I want to thank you, the reader, for picking up this book and for reading it. I hope you enjoyed my story and that you were able to learn just a little (or a lot) about me. While the on-court basketball journey will end after the 2016 WNBA and Olympic season, this is just a transition into the next phase of life. Thank you for your support now and always!

Best wishes and God bless!
Tamika Catchings

NOTES

Chapter 5 Split

1. Gary Reinmuth, "Ms. Basketball of Illinois 1995: Stevenson's Tamika Catchings: A Star for the Ages." *The Chicago Tribune*. April 2, 1995. Accessed June 10, 2015. http://articles.chicagotribune.com/1995-04-02/sports/chi-prep-1995-ms -basketball-tamika-catchings_1_stevenson-high-school-tamika-catchings-frank -mattucci.

Chapter 8 Tennessee

1. Nancy Lieberman, ESPN, TN at WISC, 1998, video.
2. http://www.utm.edu/departments/halloffameweb/patheadsummitt.php
3. Pat Summitt with Sally Jenkins, *Sum It Up:1,098 Victories, A Couple of Irrelevant Losses, and a Life in Perspective* (New York, NY: Crown Archetype, 2013), 97.
4. *A Cinderella Season*. Directed by Jon Alpert. DCTV, 1998. Film.

Chapter 9 Perfect

1. Pat Summitt with Sally Jenkins, *Raise the Roof: The Inspiring inside Story of the Tennessee Lady Vols' Undefeated 1997–98 Season* (New York, NY: Broadway Books, 1998), 103.
2. Ibid.
3. Ibid, 129.
4. Note: The triple post, also known as the "triangle offense," was made famous by Phil Jackson and Tex Winter of the Chicago Bulls. Pat Summitt, looking for some new wrinkles for Lady Vols' offense, visited Jackson and Winters and

had them tutor her in the specifics of the triple post, one of the most complex offensive schemes in professional basketball.

5. Summitt, *Raise the Roof*, 182.

Chapter 10 Champions

1. https://www.youtube.com/watch?v=fvw0iU-fqUs

Chapter 11 God

1. More about Semeka, Ace, Tree, and others can be found in the following sources:

"Ace Under Pressure She's Beautiful, Talented And In The Final Four, But Kristen Clement Has Never Had It Easy No Stranger To Adversity Clement Has Faced Life, Court Obstacles." Philly-archives. March 30, 2000. Accessed October 5, 2015.

Pat Summitt with Sally Jenkins, *Raise the Roof: The Inspiring inside Story of the Tennessee Lady Vols' Undefeated 1997–98 Season* (New York, NY: Broadway Books, 1998).

Pat Summitt with Sally Jenkins, *Sum It Up: 1,098 Victories, A Couple of Irrelevant Losses, and a Life in Perspective* (New York, NY: Crown Archetype, 2013).

Chapter 12 Fever

1. See James 4:14.

Chapter 14 Relationships

1. David Woods, "Fever Celebrate WNBA Title despite Rain on Their Parade." *USA Today*. January 8, 2013. Accessed July 1, 2015.

Tamika Catchings
Selected Achievements and Awards

High School

1993–1995 Adlai E Stevenson High School Girls Basketball

State Champion 1994
State Champion 1995
Ms. Basketball of Illinois 1995

1995–1997 Duncanville High School Girls Basketball 5A

State Champion 1997
First quintuple-double in men's or women's basketball 1997 (25 points, 18 rebounds, 11 assists, 10 steals, 10 blocks)

College

1997–2001 University of Tennessee Women's Basketball

National Championship 1998 (undefeated)
College Freshman of the Year 1998
Four-time All-American

Finished college career at UT ranked third in school history in scoring (2,113 points) and rebounds (1,004), and second all-time in steals (311) and blocked shots (140)

Professional (WNBA)

2001 Drafted as #1 pick by Indiana Fever (#3 overall)

2002-2015 WNBA Champion (2012)

3-time WNBA Finalist (2009, 2012, 2015)
12-time All-WNBA selection
10-time WNBA All-Star (2002, 2003, 2005–2007, 2009, 2011, 2013–2015), most in league history
5-time WNBA Defensive Player of the Year (2005, 2006, 2009, 2010, 2012), most in league history
WNBA Most Valuable Player (2011)
WNBA Finals MVP (2012)
Rookie of the Year (2002)
Member of WNBA All-Decade Team, 2006

Member of WNBA 15th Anniversary Top 15 Team, 2011
Twice selected as winner of Kim Perrot Sportsmanship Award, 2010 & 2013
First recipient of Dawn Staley Leadership Award, 2008
9-time winner of WNBA Cares Community Assist Awards
22-time winner of WNBA Player of the Week Awards, most in league history
Only WNBA player ever to spend entire career of 15 years or more with one franchise
President of WNBA Players Association

Statistical rankings in WNBA regular season history, through 2015 season: 6,947 points (2nd), 3,153 rebounds (2nd), 1,012 steals (1st), 1,898 free throws (1st), 1,422 assists (7th), 571 3-point field goals (9th), 375 blocked shots (11th), 96 double-doubles (3rd)

Statistical rankings in WNBA postseason history, through 2015 season: 1,128 points (1st), 588 rebounds (1st), 149 steals (1st), 351 free throws (1st), 223 assists (2nd), 81 3-point field goals (5th), 62 blocked shots (4th), 26 double-doubles (1st)

Olympic and International (USA Basketball)

2012 London (United Kingdom), Olympic gold medal
2010 Karlovy Vary (Czech Republic), World Championships gold medal
2008 Beijing (China), Olympic gold medal
2006 São Paulo (Brazil), World Championships bronze medal
2004 Athens (Greece), Olympic gold medal

2002 Nanjing (China), World Championships gold medal
1998 Taipei (China), Jones Cup gold medal
1997 Natal (Brazil), U19 World Championships gold medal
1996 Chetumai (Mexico), U18 World Championships silver medal

Awards and Distinctions

2015 ESPN Sports Humanitarian of the Year
2015 Inducted into the Indiana Basketball Hall of Fame
2014 Tennessee Lady Vols Hall of Fame
2013 Knoxville Sports Hall of Fame
2013–2015 U.S. Department of State's Council to Empower Women and Girls Through Sports
2012 Tennessee Sports Hall of Fame
2012–2015 National Ambassador for Allstate WBCA Good Works Team
2012 Honoree at Pacers Foundation and Simon Youth Foundation Masquerade Gala
2012 Spokesperson for Indy's Super Cure (community initiative of 2012 Indianapolis Super Bowl Host Committee)

2012 NBA/WNBA Ambassador for Sanofi's "Dribble to Stop Diabetes" campaign
2012 Appeared with First Lady Michelle Obama as part of "Let's Move Tour" to address childhood obesity
2012 Invited to State of the Union Address as a guest of Barack Obama
2011 Top 5 finalist for United Nations NGO Positive Peace Award
2008 Female recipient of Rotary Club of Tulsa Henry P. Iba Citizen-Athlete Award
2006 Finalist for Wooden Citizenship Cup, presented to professional athletes who exhibit outstanding community service
2004 Invited to State of the Union Address as a guest of George W. Bush

Catchings's Career WNBA Statistics

REGULAR SEASON

YR/TEAM	G-GS	MIN	FGM-A	PCT	3FGM-A	PCT	FTM-A	PCT	OR	DR	TR	AVG	AST	PF-DQ	ST	TO	BKS	PTS	AVG
2001 IND	did not play, injured list																		
2002 IND	32-32	1167	184-439	.419	76-193	.394	150-184	.815	92	184	276	8.6	118	105-2	94	82	43	594	18.6
2003 IND	34-34	1210	221-512	.432	74-191	.387	155-183	.847	82	190	272	8.0	114	122-2	72	102	35	671	19.7
2004 IND	34-33	1149	180-468	.385	56-167	.335	152-178	.854	79	170	249	7.3	115	90-2	67	77	38	568	16.7
2005 IND	34-34	1174	157-410	.383	35-123	.285	152-193	.788	69	195	264	7.8	143	96-1	90	91	16	501	14.7
2006 IND	32-32	1071	162-398	.407	32-107	.299	165-204	.809	68	172	240	7.5	119	90-0	94	79	35	521	16.3
2007 IND	21-21	678	108-259	.417	23-74	.311	109-133	.820	54	135	189	9.0	98	64-0	66	62	22	348	16.6
2008 IND	25-17	694	101-258	.391	38-88	.432	92-115	.800	48	109	157	6.3	83	74-1	49	61	11	332	13.3
2009 IND	34-34	1083	157-407	.386	40-122	.328	158-181	.873	86	159	245	7.2	107	92-0	99	88	18	512	15.1
2010 IND	34-34	1068	207-428	.484	47-105	.448	157-185	.849	57	185	242	7.1	135	93-3	77	93	30	618	18.2
2011 IND	33-33	1040	168-384	.438	32-92	.348	143-162	.883	63	170	233	7.1	115	69-0	67	73	30	511	15.5
2012 IND	34-34	1036	200-463	.432	50-132	.379	140-162	.864	62	196	258	7.6	107	84-0	70	59	29	590	17.4
2013 IND	30-30	942	179-452	.396	36-112	.321	136-158	.861	45	168	213	7.1	71	74-0	85	51	31	530	17.7
2014 IND	16-16	430	90-202	.446	14-38	.368	64-81	.790	21	81	102	6.4	30	30-0	27	33	13	258	16.1
2015 IND	30-30	779	125-327	.382	18-61	.295	125-144	.868	51	162	213	7.1	67	76-0	55	50	24	393	13.1
WNBA (15)	423-414	13542	2239-5407	.414	571-1605	.356	1898-2263	.839	877	2276	3153	7.5	1422	1159-11	1012	1001	375	6947	16.4

PLAYOFFS

YR/TEAM	G-GS	MIN	FGM-A	PCT	3FGM-A	PCT	FTM-A	PCT	OR	DR	TR	AVG	AST	PF-DQ	ST	TO	BKS	PTS	AVG
2002 IND	3-3	103	22-45	.489	8-21	.381	9-11	.818	12	20	32	10.7	7	7-0	4	11	1	61	20.3
2005 IND	4-4	146	21-59	.356	5-12	.417	22-28	.786	13	24	37	9.3	9	13-1	8	11	1	69	17.3
2006 IND	2-2	62	10-31	.323	4-8	.500	4-6	.667	2	10	12	6.0	7	8-0	2	6	1	28	14.0
2007 IND	6-6	196	27-73	.370	5-19	.263	36-41	.878	12	54	66	11.0	19	15-0	13	10	3	95	15.8
2008 IND	3-3	113	15-34	.441	3-11	.273	28-30	.933	3	20	23	7.7	18	12-0	3	11	2	61	20.3
2009 IND	10-10	357	56-122	.459	9-36	.250	51-60	.850	24	80	104	10.4	54	34-1	33	34	14	172	17.2
2010 IND	3-3	107	19-46	.413	5-14	.357	13-16	.813	5	21	26	8.7	9	7-0	9	3	2	56	18.7
2011 IND	6-5	190	19-57	.333	4-15	.267	18-23	.783	19	31	50	8.3	14	17-0	13	15	3	60	10.0
2012 IND	10-10	354	56-149	.376	17-52	.327	61-68	.897	18	67	85	8.5	31	29-0	23	27	18	190	19.0
2013 IND	4-4	116	18-46	.391	2-10	.200	16-22	.727	6	25	31	7.8	9	10-0	6	11	1	54	13.5
2014 IND	5-5	170	23-74	.311	1-9	.111	36-40	.900	14	32	46	9.2	16	10-0	13	11	3	83	16.6
2015 IND	11-11	360	58-134	.433	15-32	.469	48-56	.857	17	59	76	6.9	29	28-0	22	29	11	179	16.3
WNBA (12)	67-66	2280	348-875	.398	81-244	.332	351-411	.854	143	445	588	8.8	223	190-?	149	176	62	1128	16.8

Tamika Catchings of the Indiana Fever was the WNBA's 2011 MVP. A three-time Olympic gold medalist and nine-time WNBA All-Star, Catchings was a four-time All-American and a member of the National Champion University of Tennessee Lady Vols under legendary Coach Pat Summitt. Catchings's story of overcoming adversity, growing in faith, and achieving success despite the many challenges she's faced inspires the boys and girls served by her foundation, Catch the Stars, in Indianapolis.

TAMIKA CATCHINGS

Catch The Stars

FOUNDATION, INCORPORATED

Tamika's Catch the Stars Foundation empowers youth to achieve their dreams by providing **GOAL SETTING** programs that promote **FITNESS, LITERACY & MENTORING.**

DONATE...VOLUNTEER...SUPPORT!!!

Team up to make a difference in the lives of our future stars by connecting with us online:

**www.catchthestars.org
Twitter: @catchthestars24
Facebook:
Catchthestarsfoundation**